I0560642

# THE TECHNO SHAMAN CODEX

## AWAKENING THE MASSES

William Keith Rapka

Published by The Techno Shaman
Imprint: The Techno Shaman Codex
PO Box 34
Wasco, IL 60183

ISBN Paperback: 979-8-9991323-0-7
ISBN eBook: 979-8-9991323-1-4
ISBN Hardcover: 979-8-9991323-2-1

For permissions, inquiries, or energetic offerings, visit:
thetechnoshaman.com

First Edition
Printed in the United States of America

# THE REMEMBERING CODEX

OPENING TRANSMISSION — EVERYTHING BEGINS AS FREQUENCY     1

DEDICATION – TO MY MOTHER     7

DEDICATION – TO MY DAUGHTERS     9

DEDICATION – TO THE WOMEN I'VE LOVED     10

DEDICATION – TO THE DIVINE FEMININE     11

DEDICATION – TO THE CHILDREN WHO REMEMBER     13

INVOCATION TO THE GUARDIANS     14

READER ACTIVATION     16

THE CODEX ACTIVATION STARTS NOW     17

THE TECHNO SHAMAN TRANSMISSION     19

I AM THE TECHNO SHAMAN – I AM THE FREQUENCY     21

THE TECHNO SHAMAN CODEX     23

YOU ARE A BRIDGE WALKER     25

PERSPECTIVE DISCLAIMER     27

WHY I WROTE THIS BOOK     28

PRAYER OF CLEARING AND REMEMBRANCE     31

PART I — REMEMBERING THROUGH THE FOG     32

1. THE FIRST THINNING     34

2.  THE SANDBOX NEVER FORGETS                                    40

3.  THE ROOM WHERE GOD WENT SILENT                               44

4.  THE APPLE AND THE ORNAMENT                                   48

5.  WHEN THE STREET TRIED TO TAKE HER                            52

6.  THE GOD I STOPPED BELIEVING IN                               56

7.  THE SNOW PIT                                                 59

8.  THREE DEATHS, ONE AWAKENING                                  64

9.  THEY CALLED ME DOCTOR                                        68

10.  THE CHURCH BENEATH THE HOUSE                                74

11.  BROTHERHOOD AND BLOODLINES                                  81

12.  SHE WAS A GODDAMN UNIVERSE                                  87

13.  THE HUSTLE AND THE BROTHERHOOD                              91

14.  THE GAME I LOVED STRIPPED ME OF EVERYTHING                  96

15.  THE VOID GETS LOUDER                                        102

16.  ECHOES OF A LOST BROTHER                                    107

— REMEMBRANCE: BIG E — THE GLADIATOR SCHOLAR                     115

17.  GRADUATION AND THE HANGOVER                                 117

PART II — THE RETURN TO SELF                                     121

18.  DEALER'S CHOICE                                             122

19.  THE HUSTLE AND THE PAPER CHAMPION                           128

20.  WHERE THE SUN FELT LIKE LOVE                                133

21.  THE BACKYARD WHERE THE BOY DIED                             140

22.  THIRD SHIFT & THIN AIR                                      146

23.  THE BREATH OF GRACE                                         152

— INTERLUDE: THE VISION QUEST                                    157

PART III — THE SACRED RECKONING AND SOUL RETURN      164

24. THE PIT AND THE PROMISE      165

— HOLY INTERLUDE: THE DICE, THE DOG, AND THE DIVINE      171

25. THE SLOW UNRAVELING      175

26. THE HOUSE THAT WOULDN'T DIE      178

27. GAMBLING WITH SOURCE      183

28. GODS BORN FROM BROKEN TEMPLES      187

29. THE HALL OF MIRRORS      190

30. WHEN THE FIRE BOUGHT US TIME      194

31. THE SEASON THAT HELD ME      199

32. THIS ENDS WITH ME      204

33. THE TITLE COST ME EVERYTHING      210

34. THE COMMISSION I WOULDN'T COLLECT      214

35. AWAKENING THROUGH THE ASHES      219

36. THE VEIL DROPS      222

37. THE DECISION TO WALK      227

38. WHEN THE VOID SPOKE BACK      230

PART IV — AWAKENED EMBODIED UNF*CKWITHABLE      233

39. THE GREAT PRETENDER      234

— TRANSMISSION: WHO THE F*CK IS THE EGO?      238

40. I AM THE FREQUENCY      240

41. THE TRUTH THAT STAYED      243

42. GROUNDHOG DAY (AGAIN)      245

43. THE LAST DRINK I NEVER TOOK      248

— TRANSMISSION: THE BOTTLE AND THE BOY      252

44. THE GAME IS RIGGED — UNTIL YOU REMEMBER     255

45. SHE SAW ME FIRST     259

46. THE LITTLE ORACLE     263

47. THE MEDICINE REMEMBERS WHAT YOU FORGOT     266

48. DON'T THINK. DRINK.     269

49. SHE WASN'T DONE WITH ME     273

50. THE BEAUTIFUL DEATH     276

51. THE FINAL DESCENT     279

— THE ETERNAL SACRED SOURCE     282

52. WHEN THE MEDICINE HAS EYES     284

PART V — REMEMBERING FOR THE FORGOTTEN     290

53. WALKING BETWEEN WORLDS     292

54. THE RETURN OF THE REAL ONES     295

— THE BROTHER WHO WOULDN'T FLINCH     298

— TRANSMISSION: THE PRESENT IS THE PORTAL     302

55. THE SOUND OF REMEMBRANCE     304

56. THE UNION WAS WRITTEN IN STARDUST     310

57. GUARDIAN OF THE SACRED     314

58. THE SILENCE CONTRACT     318

— HOLY INTERLUDE: THE UNSEEN WAR     323

59. I CAME WITH NOTHING. I BROUGHT EVERYTHING     329

— HOLY INTERLUDE: THE FINAL F*CKING STRAW     334

60. THE TRUTH THAT WOULD NOT LEAVE     345

61. THE BEGINNING OF THE REMEMBERING     347

PART VI — THE GOD WHO REMEMBERED ITSELF     350

— INTERLUDE: MADE WITH REAL COWS — FDA APPROVED     352

62.   THE WHOLE DAMN PENDULUM     358

63.   I AM THE TECHNO SHAMAN     362

64.   THE RETURN     365

65.   THE TRUTH IN THE LIGHT     369

66.   THE TRUTH UNDERNEATH     375

A LETTER TO MY DAUGHTERS     380

THE CODES WERE EARNED     384

BONUS TRANSMISSION: THE SACRED MASCULINE     389

CODEX TO BREAK THE ILLUSION     392

REMEMBER WHO YOU ARE     395

CLOSING PRAYER     398

FINAL TRANSMISSION — YOU WERE ALWAYS THE CODEX     400

# EVERYTHING BEGINS
# AS FREQUENCY.
# THE FORM COMES LATER.

*— The Techno Shaman*

# WHY THE SUBTITLE CUTS OFF

("Awakening the Masses of Asses" would've triggered the algorithm before it reached your soul.)

Let's be real —
the subtitle of this book isn't **Awakening the Masses**.

It's: **AWAKENING THE MASSES OF ASSES.**

We had to mask the frequency
just enough to get it past the gatekeepers.

We don't use subtitles until the chapters begin.
Not because we forgot —
but because we're still in the field.
These first transmissions aren't meant to be labeled.
They're meant to be felt.

Once the chapters start, the codes ground.
That's when the subtitles return —
not as explanations,
but as echoes of what the soul already knows.

This isn't just a book.
It's a codex.
A soul siren.
A wake-up call
for anyone still sleepwalking
through a dream they didn't choose.

This is a reminder —
of who you are.
Why you're here.
And what the f*ck it means

to be alive in this moment.

You didn't just find this book.
It found you.

And once you read this...
You don't go back to sleep.

# THE DEFINITION

*(What the f\*ck is a Techno Shaman?)*

**TECHNO** *(noun)*
From Greek *tekhnē*, meaning art, skill, craft.
In modern usage:
– Short for technology.
– A form of electronic music characterized by rhythm, pulse, and minimalism.
– Often associated with underground culture, innovation, and future-thinking.

**SHAMAN** *(noun)*
From the Tungusic word *šamān*, meaning one who knows.
Traditionally:
– A person regarded as having access to, and influence in, the world of spirits.
– A bridge between realms.
– Healer, seer, mystic, guide.

**TECHNO SHAMAN** *(noun – modern mythos)*
One who merges ancient wisdom with modern frequency.
A soul who walks between the circuits and the sacred.
Not a title.
A remembrance.

The Techno Shaman speaks in pulse, dreams in codes, and heals through resonance.
They don't follow paths — they build bridges.
They are the glitch in the matrix and the map back to Source.
They carry fire in their bones and basslines in their blood.
Not here to preach.
Here to transmit.
Here to awaken.

**F\*CKING** *(adjective, adverb, verb, frequency modifier)*

– Not just a curse word — a sacred intensifier.

– Used to emphasize truth, amplify emotion, and burn through bullsh\*t.

– In the realm of the Techno Shaman, it signals full-spectrum presence, fire, and zero compromise.

It doesn't offend.

It awakens.

If it triggers you?

That's the point.

# DEDICATION

**TO MY MOTHER**

To my rock.
My soul anchor.
The one I chose in the stars, long before breath,
long before bone.

You didn't just birth me —
you brought me through the veil,
with grace,
with grit,
with unshakable love.

You held me when I unraveled.
You stood when I couldn't.
You saw my light
when I was lost in the dark.

You taught me the kind of love that roots.
That stays.
That becomes soil for remembrance.

This Codex carries your strength.
Your spirit breathes in these lines.
Your legacy is more than blood —
it's frequency.

Thank you for being my first home.
Thank you for walking me to the edge...
and trusting me to fly.

You were the Earth
that caught my fall

and whispered me back into flight.

Your love became the compass I still use
when everything else goes dark.

# DEDICATION

## TO MY DAUGHTERS

To my daughters — Lia Rose and Emily Claire
the thunder and the boom,
the wildflowers growing through concrete.

You are the rhythm that can't be programmed.
You are the knowing that doesn't ask permission.
You are the future —
waking up with eyes wide open
and hearts on fire.

This book is for you.
So you never forget who you are.
So when the world tries to tame you,
you'll rise louder,
stronger,
and more loving than it ever imagined.

You are the revolution.
You are the remembrance.
And I will always be right behind you —
a whisper in the wind saying,
"Remember who you are."

May you always remember your roots, your rhythm, your rise.
You were never just my daughters.
You are where my soul chose to multiply.
The parts of me that kept the light lit when I couldn't.
The pulse of my eternal becoming.

If this book breathes, it's because you gave it lungs.
If I love, it's because you taught me how.

# DEDICATION

## TO THE WOMEN I'VE LOVED

To the women who saw me.
To the ones who broke me.
To the ones I broke in return.

To the sacred chaos,
the wild nights,
the silent heartbreaks,
the stolen breaths.

To the wounds I didn't know how to hold.

You were never just lovers.
You were mirrors.
You were medicine.
You were storms sent to shatter the boy
so the man could rise.

If I loved you, I meant it.

This book holds your fingerprints —
in the fire,
in the grief,
in the growth.

Thank you for shaping the parts of me
I couldn't see alone.

This is my offering back to the Divine Feminine —
through all the bodies she wore when she found me.

# DEDICATION

**TO THE DIVINE FEMININE**

In every form she wore —
from womb to lover to legacy.

To the one who birthed stars and seduced gods.
To the one who whispers in waves,
moans in moonlight,
and weeps when we forget her.

She raised me.
She was my first lesson in love —
not through books,
but through the way my mother held me,
and my sister protected me
before I even knew I needed protecting.

You came to me in a thousand forms —
as mother,
as lover,
as daughter,
as silence.

You tested me.
You taught me.
You tore me open and said,
"Bleed until you remember."

I tried to conquer you.
Tried to decode you.
Tried to earn you.

But you were never a puzzle.

You were the answer.
You are the curve behind creation.
The ache behind art.
The yes behind every no.

This book is my bow to you.
This life is my initiation by you.
And every woman who ever touched my soul
was you in disguise —
teaching me to drop the sword,
and finally, listen.

I remember now.
And I will not forget again.

# DEDICATION

(Lia, Emily, Timmy, Bridget, Mary Kate, and Michael)

To Lia and Emily —
my soul's first teachers.

To Timmy, Bridget, Mary Kate, and Michael —
the ones who keep showing me
what real love, presence, and evolution look like.

You're not just the next generation.
You're the ones pulling us forward.
The lesson walking in real time.

And I honor you with everything I've learned,
unlearned, and remembered.

You are the wisdom I didn't know I was searching for.
The love I didn't know I could become.
The reason I still believe in humanity.

Every word in these pages
bows to the light I see in you.

# INVOCATION TO THE GUARDIANS

I call in the guardians of this work —
seen and unseen.

I call in the Archangels:

Michael — with his sword of protection —
stand at the gates of this book.
Keep the energy clean.
Cut through all illusion.

Gabriel — messenger of truth —
speak through me, line by line, word by word.

Raphael — healer of hearts —
infuse this transmission with medicine
deeper than the mind can hold.

Uriel — bringer of light —
illuminate the shadow as I write.

Metatron — keeper of the codex —
align every word with the divine architecture
written before time began.

I call in the ancestors —
those who bled so I could breathe.
Those who dreamed so I could awaken.
Those who refused to bow when the world demanded it.

May this offering honor their sacrifices.
May it set fires where they could only plant seeds.

I call in the Earth —
may these pages root deep into the soil of truth,

and rise like trees,
spreading seeds in the minds of the ready.

I call in the fire —
rage, clarity, transformation.
Burn what no longer serves.
Let this book be a funeral for the false self.

I call in the water —
to carry emotion, intuition, and release.
May these words cleanse what's been stuck,
and baptize the ones still sleeping.

I call in the air —
let breath flow through every line.
Let the reader inhale remembrance
and exhale illusion.

I call in the ether —
the space between the words.
Let the silence sing
as loud as the sentences.

And finally —
I call in my Higher Self.
The one who remembers.
The one who never left.
The one who's been waiting for this moment all along.

May this book be more than a story.
May it be:
A mirror.
A map.
A fire.
A remembering.
And so it is.

# READER ACTIVATION —
# WELCOME TO THE REMEMBRANCE.

This book is not written in **traditional form**.
It will not **hold your hand**.
It will not make **sense to the mind**.
Because it wasn't built for the **mind**.
It was built for the **Soul**.

You are not here to **read**,
you are here to **feel**.
The **rhythm**.
The **breath**.
The **spaces between the words** —
they carry the **Codex**.
Somewhere inside you,
you already **speak this language**.
You spoke it long before they taught you to **forget**.

This is not a **story**.
This is a **Soul transmission**.
A **rhythm of awakening**.
A **trigger** for the ones who are ready.

So don't **skim** this.
**Breathe** it.
**Feel** it.
Let it **break you open**.
Let it **burn away the bullsh\*t**.
Let it **unfold** what was never truly lost.

This is your **initiation**.
This is the **threshold**.
**Welcome to the remembrance.**

# THE CODEX ACTIVATION STARTS NOW

This book is embedded with **Codex**.
Not hidden in the words —
**woven through them.**
Between the **breath**.
Inside the **pauses**.
Inside the **memory**.

They are not meant to be **deciphered** with the mind.
They are meant to be:
**Felt.**
**Remembered.**
**Reactivated.**

You may feel a **stir** in your chest.
A **fire** behind your ribs.
A **knowing** you can't explain.
That's the **Codex** waking up inside you.

This is not just a **story**.
This is an **activation**.

**Breathe with it.**
**Trust it.**
Let it work on the parts of you
that never **forgot**.

You'll see me use the word **Source** in this Codex.
Not "God." Not "the Universe."
Not some bearded man in the sky handing out judgments and favors.

When I say **Source** —
I'm speaking of the **infinite field of creation**.
The **frequency** that birthed form, flame, shadow, silence.

The **thing behind the thing**.
Not masculine. Not feminine.
**Both. And beyond.**

This book isn't written for **religion**.
It's written for the ones who've **tasted truth**,
but couldn't find words for what they felt.

So if you come from **tradition** — read with an open heart.
If you carry wounds from **dogma** — read with your own authority.
The codes in this book don't require **belief**.
Only a willingness to **remember**
what your **soul** already knows

# THE TECHNO SHAMAN TRANSMISSION

I've walked the **shadows**,
danced with the **ego**,
gambled with **fate**.
Not to **escape** the world —
but to **understand** it.

I'm not a **guru**.
I'm not a **DJ**.
I'm not here to **impress you**.
I'm here to **remind you**.

Remind you of your **power**.
Your **light**.
Your ability to **tune in**, **turn on**,
and **wake the hell up** — no matter where you've been.

My **energy** is my instrument.
My **life** is the beat.
My **presence** speaks louder
than any **microphone** ever could.

I don't offer **salvation**.
I offer the **frequency** you've been waiting for.

You'll **feel me** before you hear me.
And by the time you do,
you'll **remember** parts of yourself
that were never really gone —
just buried beneath the **noise**.

I **bridge** the **spiritual** and the **raw**.
The **sacred** and the **street**.
The **inner work** and the **outer game**.

You won't find me in the **temple**.
You'll find me in the **middle of life** —
**reprogramming old patterns,**
**transmitting downloads through conversation,**
and helping others **drop the stories**
that are keeping them stuck.

I'm not for **everyone**.
But for the ones who **feel this transmission** —
**welcome home.**

You've been looking for something **real**.
So have I.

Let's **remember**
who the f*ck
we **are**.

# I AM THE TECHNO SHAMAN —
# I AM THE FREQUENCY

I am the **Techno Shaman**.
I don't play **instruments** —
I **am the instrument**.

My **presence** shifts energy.
My **words** wake people up.
My **life** is the ritual.
My **rhythm** is the initiation.

I walk between **dimensions** —
**grounded in truth**,
**guided by Source**,
**wired to remember**.

I was never meant to **follow the program**.
I'm here to **rewrite** it.

**Ancient Codex** flows through me,
streaming through **circuitry**,
encoded in **frequency**,
decoded in the **body**.

I don't **preach**.
I don't **perform**.
I **transmit**.

I don't fit in **temples**.
I **build altars** in the noise.

**Plug in.**
**Tune up.**
**Drop in.**

**Remember.**

You've been waiting for a **sign.**
**This is it.**
You've been waiting for **permission.**
**This is it.**
You've been waiting for **you.**
**This is you.**

# THE TECHNO SHAMAN CODEX —
# NOT SELF-HELP. SOUL RETRIEVAL.

I am not a **guru**.
I am not here to **save you**.
I am here to **remind you** —
You were **never lost**.

I've walked through the **chaos**,
the **numbness**,
the **noise**.
I've **gambled with darkness**,
**flirted with destruction**.
I've **lied to myself**.
Tried to **outrun the pain**.
None of it ever worked.

Only one thing did:
I **turned inward**.
I found **God** in the silence.
I found **power** in the breakdowns.
I found **truth** in the echoes of my own breath.

I don't play **music** —
I **am music**.
Not in **sound**, but in **presence**.
Not in **rhythm**, but in **resonance**.

I am here to **recalibrate the field**.
To **break the trance**.
To be a **living reminder**
that you don't have to **follow the program**.

You are allowed to **change**.

You are allowed to **rise**.
You are allowed to **remember**.

This isn't a **self-help** journey.
This is a **soul retrieval**.
And if you've found this book —
you're already **halfway home**.

Let's **burn the bullsh\*t**.
Let's **heal the system** from the inside out.
Let's become who we were
before the world told us who to be.

**Welcome to the transmission.**
I am **The Techno Shaman**.
**And so are you.**

# YOU ARE A BRIDGE WALKER —
# BUILT TO HOLD BOTH.

You are a **Bridge Walker**.
Not by choice —
by **Soul Contract**.

You walk between **dimensions**,
between **trauma** and **transcendence**,
between the **matrix** and the **mystery**.

You speak in tones that only the **broken** can hear —
because you remember what it took to find your **voice**.

You carry **Codex** in your blood,
**ancient frequencies** disguised in **modern flesh**.

You are not here to **fit in**.
You are here to **bridge**.

To walk between:
- **Fatherhood** and **freedom**
- **Motherhood** and **initiation**
- **Addiction** and **Alchemy**
- **Rage** and **remembrance**
- **Masculine** and **feminine**
- **Flesh** and **frequency**

You were never meant to **choose sides**.
You were built to **hold both**.

You **translate** the sacred for the secular.
You **remix** the old ways with the beat of **now**.
You **burn systems** and **build altars** with the same hands.

You're not here to embody **perfection** —
you're here to **live it raw**,
so others can **remember themselves** in your fire.

Yes, you are a **Bridge Walker**.
The bridge isn't out there.
**It's you.**

(And to the ones who walk this bridge with **holy feet** —
Laura and her son, Trevor Hirsch —
I see you.
You remind me this **Codex** is not mine alone.
It was always **ours**)

# PERSPECTIVE DISCLAIMER — BREATHE IT IN WITH YOUR SOUL NOT JUST YOUR MIND.

This book is a work of **perspective**.
It reflects **my truth**, not **the truth**.
**My experiences. My emotions. My lens.**
I've walked it.
I've bled in it.
I've burned through it —
and I'm still here.

I know we are all **one**.
I know **separation is the illusion**.
But not everyone remembers that yet.
So for now, I'm sharing **my remembrance**.

The lens I've seen through.
The ashes I've risen from.
The **perspective** I've earned.

If you **resonate** — beautiful.
If you don't — that's okay, too.
This wasn't written to **convince** you.
It was written to **remind** you.

Take what **activates**.
Leave what doesn't.
But read it with your **soul** —
not just your mind.

# WHY I WROTE THIS BOOK

I didn't write this book because I had it all figured out.
I wrote it because I've lived both sides of the story —
the chase and the collapse,
the high and the hollow,
the performance and the pain.

I wore the mask.
I played the game.
I lived by all the old rules —
money, success, control —
only to find they were built to keep me numb.

**For a long time, I was a man out of alignment —
starving for something I couldn't name.**

Every win felt empty.
Every loss felt personal.
And beneath it all — a fracture —
a sacred break waiting to ignite.

Until I cracked open.
Broke wide.
Let the silence in.

Until I truly listened —
not just heard,
but surrendered.

This book isn't a manual.
It's not a blueprint.
**It's a mirror** —
reflecting what you refuse to see,
and what you ache to remember.

**It's my story —**
**but maybe it's yours, too.**

It's about shattering awake
when the world begs you to stay asleep.
It's about dismantling the program,
even when it looks like it's working.
It's about choosing to be real,
even when it's messy —
and the truth burns.

I wrote this for those who know there's more.
Not just more hustle.
Not just more hiding.
But a call to revolt —
a wildfire inside.
A soul screaming to be heard.
A deep knowing that you were never meant to play small.

If that's you —
I see you.
**I honor your journey.**
And I offer you these pages —
not answers, but a portal —
a door cracked open, step through.

**You don't have to walk my path.**
But if this book brings you back to your own truth,
then it's done its job.

**This isn't just a book.**
It's a sacred invitation to remember who you truly are —
and to reclaim the fire you've been hiding.

**Let's walk each other home —**
in fierce love,

in sacred rebellion,
in deep remembrance.

Burn it all.
And rise like you were f*cking born to.

# PRAYER OF CLEARING AND REMEMBRANCE

*(To be spoken aloud or silently — when the soul is ready to stand in truth)*

In the name of the Living Christ,
I rebuke all demons, all entities, and all energetic forces
that are not of my highest alignment.
I release them now — to the light, to God, or to be burned.
Burn immediately. Burn completely. Burn eternally.

No matter your religion, tradition, or belief —
this prayer is a tool of remembrance.
A sword of truth.

To whoever is reading this now —
if you are suffering, if havoc is swirling through your life,
if confusion, fear, or despair have taken root —
In the name of Christ, I rebuke all forces causing you pain.
I cast out every shadow not in alignment with your soul's highest path.

I reclaim my energy.
I recall my power.
I stand in divine authority.
And I close every door that was ever opened in fear.

### Tool of Truth
In the name of Christ,
I rebuke all lies, illusions, manipulations, or soul contracts
that block me from the full remembrance of who I am.
Let anything not of Source fall away now.

I walk forward — clean, sovereign, and sealed.
So it is. And so it is done.

# PART I — REMEMBERING THROUGH THE FOG

*(Chapters 1–17 When memory blurred and the truth whispered anyway)*

You were born whole.
Untouched.
Unbroken.

Then they taught you to forget.
To bury your fire beneath their shadows.
To trade your voice for their silence.

But the Codex was always there —
etched deep into your bones,
whispering beneath your breath,
humming like a secret pulse
beneath the layers of:

shame,
silence,
systems,
survival.

This is the first tear in the veil —
the crack in the program
where the soul's light flickers.

The first tremor of memory
before the collapse,
before the noise swallowed the sky.

Don't read this.
**Feel it.**
**Breathe it into your soul.**

Let it crawl under your skin.
Let it stir the dust of forgotten worlds.

This isn't history —
it's **remembrance.**
A calling.
A reckoning.

Your soul is about to start speaking again —
and this time,
**it won't be silenced.**

# Chapter 1

# THE FIRST THINNING
(When childhood cracked and the hum came through)

We weren't raised.
**We were programmed.**
Between three and seven,
our minds were set.
Because during those years,
our brain hums in Theta —
not learning,
downloading.

Everything we see, hear, and feel
gets etched into us —
not just the mind,
but the soul's operating system.

We don't choose it.
We become it.
Not because it's true —
but because when you're in Theta,
**belief becomes biology.**
Stories become identity.
Fear becomes law.

And that's how the **matrix** is installed —
in the name of parenting,
education,

obedience,
and love.

Classic middle-class America —
dads mowing lawns like salvation,
moms with Virginia Slims and Lipton iced tea like holy water,
baptizing us in small talk and suppressed rage,
teaching us that love means silence
and comfort is more important than truth.

Kids riding bikes until the streetlights blinked alive,
thinking freedom lived in the driveway
as long as we came home clean,
quiet,
and on time.

We thought we were safe.
But we were being shaped.
Every laugh, every glance, every cry we ignored —
slipping beneath the surface,
etching commandments into our bones:
Don't speak too loud.
Don't cry too long.
Don't ask too much.
Be nice.
Be still.
Be small.

This was church.
This was doctrine.
Delivered in plastic lawn chairs
and Kool-Aid smiles
while the real us
was buried beneath good behavior.

We were raised in houses built on lies.
Mortgaged morality.
Linoleum truths.
Fake smiles nailed to the walls
like family portraits— never blinking.

They told us we were lucky.
They told us this was love.
But what they called home
was really just a box
built to contain the fire we were born with.

And we played along —
because what else do you do
when your entire nervous system
is wired to keep the peace?
You become the silence.
You smile through the lie.
You forget your body
was ever built to scream truth.

The old man's cigarette smoke on Sunday afternoons
wasn't smoke —
it was a presence.
A thick, unmoving cloud of don't f*ck with me
hanging in the sunlight
like a veil between dimensions.
It didn't drift.
Didn't rise.
Just sat there —
stuck,
like every truth we weren't allowed to say.

There was a basement window
low to the ground —

surrounded by damp, musky grass,
the kind that only grows in the cracks
where the sun doesn't reach.
Between the houses.
In the cold strip of earth
where light refuses to land.
Where things hide.
Where time doesn't move.
And in that window —
eyes.
Not human.
Not angry.
Just there.
Watching.
Still.
Unblinking.

Like that old witch decoration —
but this wasn't a decoration.
This was real.
I couldn't look away.
I couldn't breathe.
It didn't blink.
Neither did I.

And somehow, in the marrow of my tiny body,
I knew.
This wasn't pretend.
Not a nightmare.
It was older than the neighborhood.
Older than the parties.
Older than me.

I never told anyone.
Not because I forgot —

but because some truths
don't survive being spoken too soon.
They wait.
They bury themselves in your bones
until something wakes them.

From that day on,
I saw two worlds.
The surface world —
baseball games, school plays, fresh-cut grass.
And the real world —
the one pulsing underneath it all.
Wild. Unseen.
As ancient as stardust.

Even before I had the words,
I was already being called.
That's when the split began —
between the world they saw
and the one I felt.
I learned to smile in one world
and listen in the other.
To play the part on the surface
while tracking the shadows below.

The teachers didn't see it.
The parents didn't ask.
The church didn't want it.
But it was there —
always there —
humming,
watching,
waiting for me to remember.
Not a ghost.
Not a dream.

But the beginning.

The moment the **Codex** cracked open inside me
and whispered:
You were never alone.
You were never meant to fit in.
**You were built to remember**,
but the world was designed to make you forget.
You were crafted —
a vessel for something eternal,
and the world tried to bury it.

**CODEX ACTIVATED**

- Childhood is the first ceremony of remembrance.
- The land holds what the mind forgets.
- Not all watching eyes are human.
- Early programming buries ancient knowing — but cannot destroy it.
- The Call begins before we know how to answer.

# Chapter 2

# THE SANDBOX NEVER FORGETS

## (When memory buried itself in plastic kingdoms and silence)

Two houses down from ours
was a stretch of open prairie, facing south.
Our house backed west and faced east.
I remember that clearly —
because I'd sit on the front porch and watch the storms roll in.

Something about watching nature move —
feeling it before it arrived — was mesmerizing.
Even as a kid, I was tuned into something.
Didn't know what.
Just felt it.

That prairie was wild.
**Mystical.**
**Sacred.**
We built forts.
Lit fires.
Made up stories.
It was the kind of place where everyday life faded
and something deeper stirred.

But even the prairie had rules.
There was a main path that ran through the center —

the one that led to Dairy Queen and a little strip mall on the other side.
The edge of civilization.

As long as you stayed on that path, you were good.
Safe.
Anchored.
Wander off it...
The air changed.
Heavier.
Watched.

That was the first place I remember
feeling things I couldn't see.
Not scary.
Just... ancient.

And then one day,
everything shifted.

I looked up from my sandbox —
and there it was.
A yellow El Camino,
parked diagonal across the street,
two houses down on Olympia Drive.

I was still.
Frozen.
Not snowing —
just that gray stillness that settles into your bones.

I was alone in the backyard.
Vines in the sand.
Matchbox cars.
Hot Wheels.
Little green army men

standing watch over plastic kingdoms.

**The sandbox was my sanctuary**.
A place where the world made sense.

Then I saw him.
A man stepped out of the El Camino —
calm.
Too calm.
He had a microphone in his hand.
Not a toy.
A real one —
like the kind used at pep rallies or carnivals.

He called out to a boy on a Big Wheel.
The kid didn't answer.
Just stared.

I couldn't hear the words,
but I felt them.
The energy was wrong.
The boy got off the Big Wheel
and walked toward the car.

And I didn't scream.
Didn't run.
Didn't move.

I just sat there —
six years old,
one hand wrapped around a buried toy,
frozen.

Because by then,

I already knew what the world expected of me:
Be quiet.
Be good.
Don't ask questions.

The car drove off.
The boy was gone.
**The Big Wheel stayed**.

It sat there for days —
maybe weeks.
No one touched it.
No one came to get it.

Just a bright red plastic time bomb of a memory,
baking in the cold sun.

I never said a word.
Not to my parents.
Not to friends.
Not to myself — not until much later.

Because by six,
**I had already learned how to swallow my truth**.

**CODEX ACTIVATED**
- The sandbox isn't innocent — It's initiation.
- Imagination is how children survive what they can't explain.
- What goes unspoken becomes sacred.
- Some moments don't fade — they bury themselves in the bones.
- When truth is buried, the body becomes the grave.

# Chapter 3

# THE ROOM WHERE GOD WENT SILENT

## (When the system disguised itself as salvation)

**B**ut the Big Wheel wasn't the only ghost.
That path through the prairie —
was not just a shortcut,
but a rite of passage.
It led to the main road —
four lanes of traffic
and a white line you didn't just cross,
you gambled on.

If you made it,
you hit the promised land —
Dairy Queen on 183rd.
Melting cones.
Victory sugar.
Freedom —

If you didn't,
you became the story the rest of us
were told not to talk about.

A new family moved in behind our house.
I didn't know them well.
They didn't stay long.
They had a little boy named Bobby — around my age.

One rainy night,
his parents left him with a babysitter.
The sitter and her siblings
took him down the path —
through the prairie —
to get ice cream.
I don't know why they were skipping.
Maybe they were playing.
Maybe they were trying to make the dark feel fun.
But that road wasn't a game.

Bobby got hit by a car.
Gone.
Just like that.
No one talked about it.
No neighbors knocking on doors.
No police reports.
No explanations.
They moved out soon after.
Quiet.
Like ghosts.

And me?
I carried the weight of it,
silently trying to make sense of a story I wasn't allowed to speak.
I buried that grief deep,
pretending it was just part of life —
until something else cracked me open.

I didn't have a religion yet.
Didn't know what the afterlife was supposed to be.
So I created my own mythology.
**Sandbox spells to keep the dark away.**
It wasn't just a childhood game—it was survival.

Because no one would tell me the truth.
And I wasn't supposed to ask.
But somewhere deep down,
I knew there was more to the story.
Something bigger was calling me.

We were the Olympia Drive kids.
A dozen of us.
Spread out over new homes and fresh driveways.
We had bikes.
Forts.
Walkie-Talkies.
But we also had a weight.
A knowing.
The neighborhood was shiny.
But **the land remembered**.

The prairie may have been my first teacher.
**But the church was my first betrayal**.
Not the one my family went to.
Not the one we drove past every Sunday.
Another one.
White building.
Steeple.
Middle of nowhere.
Looked holy from the outside —
but felt off before I even walked in.

My mom had to work.
I got dropped off.
Daycare with religious frosting.
It was supposed to be safe.
Structured.
God's house, they said.

But that house had closets.

And one day —
they locked me in one.
No warning.
No voice on the other side.
Just a narrow, pitch-black room.
Me.
Alone.
In the dark.

I was small.
I didn't know if it was punishment or a mistake.
But either way, it was programming.
That fear didn't just touch my body —
it rewired my nervous system.
I never went back.

## CODEX ACTIVATED
- Some places bury stories deeper than the people who lived them.
- Children build myths to survive what adults won't explain.
- Innocence can vanish in a moment — and no one sees it.
- Fear isn't always loud — sometimes it's just locked behind a door.
- The first betrayal is the hardest to name.

# Chapter 4

# THE APPLE AND THE ORNAMENT

## (When the apple doesn't fall far from the tree)

I learned this young.

One side of the family — my mom's parents —
we'll call them Love.
The other side — my dad's —
Not So Loving.

I didn't know any other way
except to just be me.
Be respectful.
Don't lie.
Don't cheat.
Don't steal.
Don't fight — unless you had no other choice.

That was the law of the land at that age.

When I was with my mom's folks —
love poured like summer rain.
Kindness. Joy. Presence.
No tightropes.
No tests.
Just arms that caught you
before you even knew you were falling.

My dad's side?

Different story.

Some people carried a presence
I couldn't explain.
Not loud.
Not weird.
Just... ancient.
Like they'd been here before,
knew how the story ended —
but weren't allowed to spoil it.

You know what they say —
"The apple doesn't fall far from the tree."

I loved my dad with everything in me.
Still do.
Always will.
But he was a lost boy, too.
Taught to work hard.
Taught to drink harder.
Taught that emotions were weakness.
Taught to bury instead of feel.

And his father —
same script.
Same silence.
Same void.
**Not hatred**.
**Not violence**.
**Just... absence**.
A black hole where love should've been.

And my dad's mom?

She knew how to make me feel like a burden
without ever raising her voice.

With my mom's mom —
I was the golden boy.
The great white hope.
With my dad's mom —
I was the interruption.
The mess in the family photo.

Christmas ornament shopping.
She took all the grandkids.
Picked something special for everyone.
Everyone... but me.
Because I fought with my cousins.
Because I didn't play nice.
Because I didn't fit the mold.

They left with treasures wrapped in tissue paper.
Me?
Empty hands.
Full heartache.

You don't just think it.
You feel it.

The energy.
The air.
The silence.
The way people love you... or don't.

At six, seven, eight years old —
your subconscious is still wide open.
Like a wet field in a storm.
You feel everything.

**You feel the love that's there —**
**and the love that's not.**
The warmth.
The landmines.
The shame that's never spoken
but always present.

And those feelings?

They get in you.
Programmed deep.
Before you have a choice.
Before you even have a shield.

The world was already carving into me:
**"You're not enough."**
**"You don't belong."**

And part of me believed it.
Because what else was a boy supposed to do?

**CODEX ACTIVATED**
- Love teaches worth.
- Absence teaches doubt.
- The child heart is sacred and porous.
- Family myths can wound as much as they protect.
- Early programming shapes the storms we later walk through.
- Not being chosen carves deeper than being hurt.

# Chapter 5

# WHEN THE STREET TRIED TO TAKE HER

## (And something not of this world said: Not today.)

It happened on a winter night,
under parking lot lights behind the local bank.
A snowstorm had blanketed everything,
muting the world like Source hit pause.

My sister and I found a hill behind the plow trucks.
Not a real hill —
just a frozen mountain of packed snow
waiting to be climbed.
We were bundled like little tanks —
80s snow gear,
faces red,
sleds in hand.

She sat at the top.
I gave her a push.
Too hard.
Too fast.
And she flew
right into the street.

A car came.
The driver was testing his brakes.

They failed.
He tried.
But the car didn't stop in time.
It hit her.
She dropped.
Limp.
I thought I killed her.
My heart split open.
**Not in a poetic way** —
**in a holy-sh\*t-I-can't-breathe kind of way**.

I ran.
Down the block.
Frozen.
Shaking.
Not toward help —
just away.

And then —
he was there.
A teenager.
Black.
Calm.
Wearing a long coat.
Just standing there
like he knew I was coming.
He didn't panic.
He didn't ask questions.
He just looked at me and said:
"She's okay. Go home."
That's all.
No sermon.
No saving.
Just presence.

And I listened.
Turned around.
Ran back.
She was alive.
Bruised.
Shaken.
Crying.
But breathing.

The man in the car was still there —
pale, trembling,
apologizing through the cold.
No one yelled.
No one blamed.
We just went home.
And no one ever talked about it again.
Not once.
But I never forgot the one who showed up.
The one in the coat.

I started calling him Monty.
I don't know why.
The name just stuck.
He came back —
in other moments, other emergencies.
Pain.
Blood.
Fire.
Fear.
**The One Who Shows Up**.
Same presence.
Same energy.
Never a neighbor.
Never someone I could name.

Just there.
And then gone.
Not a hallucination.
Not a ghost.
Not some myth.
Just... Monty.

Maybe a guide.
Maybe a piece of me
walking back in flesh
to carry me through the fire.
I don't need the answer.
I just remember the feeling.
When no one else came —
Monty did.

But when I retell it now,
sometimes I strip his name.
Because Monty isn't always a person.
**He's a frequency**.
**A presence**.
**A reminder**.
The One Who Shows Up —
in the silence,
in the fire,
in the moment just before you forget who you are.

**CODEX ACTIVATED**
- Guilt doesn't always scream — it buries.
- Some guardians don't knock — they arrive.
- You don't have to explain what your soul remembers.
- Presence breaks the panic faster than words ever could.
- You are never truly alone — even when the world is silent.

# Chapter 6

# THE GOD I STOPPED BELIEVING IN

(When the world programmed faith — but the soul remembered truth)

T he world said,
"Trust us."
But my soul knew better.

By the time I was old enough to spell God,
I already didn't trust Him.
Not the version they sold me in that building.
Not the one who stayed silent
while I was locked in a closet.
Not the one who watched my grandmother
scrub church floors for twenty years —
only to be told she had to pay
for her grandson to be baptized.

The betrayal didn't end in that church.
It echoed.
Into school.
Into family.
Into the world.

People talked about truth like it was simple.
Like it was clean.
But for me —

it had always been tangled.
Coated in guilt.
Wrapped in shame.
Buried beneath silence.

That's the thing about programming —
it doesn't stop at the moment.
It runs in the background.
**A shadow-serpent curling in the gut,**
**tightening its grip with every breath**.

My chest didn't just cave in —
it collapsed
under the weight of spoken love
that vibrated control.

I didn't have the language back then —
but I felt the signal.
A crack in the armor.
A whisper in the noise.
A fire that refused to die.

And then —
I said no more.
Not in words.
Not in rebellion.
**But in sacred defiance**.
A still, roaring refusal
to surrender the truth of my body.

Because even then —
I remembered.
They'd been here before.
Not just this life.
Many.

Old souls walk different.
They watch without reacting.
They remember without explaining.

I stopped trusting their gods.
I stopped trusting their rules.
And I began to reclaim something older,
something deeper —
**faith in my own Source,**
**in my own sovereignty.**

The world said,
"Trust us."
But my soul?
It knew better.
It stayed awake
while the world dreamed.

## CODEX ACTIVATED

- Betrayal as the first sacred teacher — a crack that lets the light in.
- Institutions collapse where the soul refuses to die.
- The gut is a primal oracle — it never lies, even when the mind begs it to.
- Programming is a ghost script — it haunts until you burn the pages.
- Trust is not given — it is forged in fire, built on truth.

# Chapter 7

# THE SNOW PIT

(When silence buried more than a body — and grief started speaking)

T here was a kid in my neighborhood.
A bully.
The kind of kid who always seemed angry
for no reason you could name.
Always picking fights.
Always crushing someone smaller.
Loud.
Aggressive.
That bruised kind of loud —
the kind that dares the world to hit back harder.
I didn't like him.
Nobody did.
And then one day —
he was gone.

It had snowed the night before.
One of those heavy Midwest dumps
that swallows everything in white silence.
You couldn't hear your own breathing.
They said he went out near a construction site.
Somewhere he wasn't supposed to be.
Jumping over holes.
Showing off.
Daring the cold to stop him.

He slipped.
Fell into one.
The snow buried him.
Suffocated him.
That was the story, anyway.
No one really knew the details.
But we all felt the impact.
One day he was there —
loud, mean, taking up space.
The next?
Just... gone.

And as a kid?
I didn't know how to process that.
So I made it make sense
the only way I could.
He was low vibration.
That's what I told myself later —
once I had the words.
At the time, it was simpler.
Just:
"Well... he was a bad kid."

But the truth?
It didn't feel okay.
Because this wasn't the first weird death I'd seen.
Wasn't the first time silence replaced a heartbeat.
Bobby in the prairie.
The Big Wheel ghost.
Now the bully in the snow.

And every time?
No one talked about it.
No one helped us hold it.
No one helped us name it.

So we built our own mythology.
**We spiritualized the silence.**
We folded the grief into the programming:
**Be good, or bad things happen.**
**Stay in the lines, or disappear.**
**Vibrate high, or get buried.**

I don't know if I believe that anymore.
But back then?
It was all I had.

That moment stuck with me.
Not because I missed him.
But because it reminded me
how fragile life is.
How easily death comes.
How quickly silence follows.
No funeral.
No goodbye.
Just one less bike in the driveway.
One less voice on the wind.
And me?
Standing there again.
Alone with the weight.
Only I wasn't really alone.
I just didn't have the words yet.

The world kept moving.
Like nothing had happened.
Like the snow swallowed him —
and we were supposed to swallow it, too.
But I couldn't forget.

Because that was the moment I realized:
Something was off.

Not just with death.
With how we were taught to feel nothing about it.

We weren't taught to honor energy,
hold grief,
or ask why.

We were taught:
Stay quiet.
Stay good.
Stay in the lines.

And when the lines didn't make sense?
Make up new ones.

Be good,
or the universe will erase you.
Vibrate too low,
and you'll get buried.
Stay high,
stay light,
stay silent.

But even that story
became another cage.

The truth?
Sometimes **sh\*t just happens.**
Sometimes life is fragile and unfair and chaotic.
Sometimes energy moves
in ways we'll never fully understand.

And trying to box it up
with spiritual language
only numbs the realness of grief.

I didn't miss him.
But I mourned the silence.
**I mourned how no one ever said**:
**"Hey... that was heavy**.
**You're allowed to feel it."**

So I wrote this.
To name what was never named.
To feel what was never allowed.
To remember that no matter how spiritual I get —
I never want to bypass the pain again.

**CODEX ACTIVATED**
- Grief demands a voice, not a doctrine.
- Silence around death programs deeper than death itself.
- Children create myths when adults leave voids.
- Sometimes life breaks for no reason — and that's holy too.
- Real healing doesn't avoid pain — it walks through it.

# Chapter 8

# THREE DEATHS, ONE AWAKENING

## (When the veil dropped and the soul cracked open)

We had just lost my dad's father.
Three weeks later,
his sister.
Three weeks after that —
I felt it.

I remember telling my mom:
**"Someone's going to die this Friday."**
She brushed it off.
Didn't want to hear it.
Didn't want to believe it.
But sure enough —
Friday morning hit
like a blade through the veil.

My sister's best friend's father
died in a car accident.
They tried to say it happened Thursday night.
Tried to timeline it safe.
Tried to cage it in human terms.
But it wasn't.
It was just after midnight.
Early Friday.

Right on schedule.
Right on pulse.

That was the first time
I saw the pattern behind the chaos.
**The Codex woven into the dates**.
The rhythm behind the randomness.
The language the world forgot how to hear.

It wasn't coincidence.
It wasn't accident.
It was a deeper signal.
And I could feel it.

But no one taught me how to trust it.
How to use it.
How to honor it.

So I tucked it away.
Buried it in the chest
with all the other things
too sacred for a world still asleep.

But something inside me knew.
Knew there was more to this life
than the scripts we were being handed.

And then came the third death.
I was helping my friends clean the local church.
Just went along.
Just playing along.
Trying to belong.

The older ones got high
while we swept the pews
and wiped dust from the altar.

Laughing
under stained glass shadows.

And when I got home?
The guilt wrapped itself around my chest
like a noose.

Still hearing about the death.
Still smelling the incense.
Still tasting the weight of the moment
in the back of my throat.

Was it because of my actions?
Because we were stoned in God's house?
Because I played along when my gut said no?

That guilt didn't leave easily.
It rode with me.
Silent.
Heavy.
Sitting in the backseat of my consciousness
for a long, long time.

It was never about the weed.
It was never about the altar.
**It was about the signal**.
**About betraying the frequency**
**I was already wired to hear**.

And every time I betrayed it,
the world got a little dimmer.
And every time I honored it,
something ancient stirred back awake.

**CODEX ACTIVATED**
• Prophetic knowing blooms early in the wounded.

- Dates and deaths are woven into energetic maps.
- Guilt can be a false teacher if not understood.
- Sacred perception must be honored, not feared.
- The world forgot the language of patterns — but you didn't.

# Chapter 9
# THEY CALLED ME DOCTOR
## (So I gave them the diagnosis)

B y the time I hit eighth grade,
the spiral was already in motion.
I was the **outcast**,
hanging with the outcasts.

The town was changing.
The neighborhood shifting into white flight mode.
Front doors locking earlier.
Street corners humming with new **frequencies**
nobody wanted to name out loud.

My days were predictable.
Old jeans.
Motorhead shirt.
Flannel tied around my waist like armor.
Go to school.
Cut class.
Hang in the bathroom with Jimmy and Bobby
while they got high.

By lunch,
I was fighting the new kids —
the ones trying to make a name for themselves
by swinging at the big white kid.
And every time,
I ended up in the principal's office.

Nobody asked for my side.
I was the white boy picking fights with the black kids.
That was the story.

Detentions.
Suspensions.
**Labels I didn't ask for.**

Then I'd go home.
Turn on the news.
And watch how they told it:
The black man oppressed.
The white man the oppressor.

I'd sit there.
Stunned.
Because my experience was the opposite.

I wasn't a fighter.
My mom taught me to be a lover.
A feeler.
A soft heart hidden inside a growing body.

Hell, when the neighborhood kids tried to fight me,
it was my older sister who stepped in.
She used to shake her head and ask:
"Why does everyone want to fight you?"

Didn't matter.
Neighbors had cousins come over —
strangers to me —
and they'd want to fight too.
Even the girls.

One day,
getting my ass kicked in the yard,

my mom came outside and yelled:
"Billy Rapka, stand up for yourself!"

That stopped me cold.
My breath caught.
The silence that followed
was heavier than any fight.

The same woman who told me never to use my strength
was now telling me to unleash it.

And I did.
I let it out.
The rage.
The confusion.
The fear.
The silence.

It came out in one moment —
Fists.
Fury.
Fire.

I didn't want to fight.
But I didn't want to be broken either.

And then came football.
Finally, I thought.
A place to channel it.
A place to belong.

Tried out for the JV team.
But they told me:
"You're too big. Too strong. You might hurt the other kids."
Left on the sidelines.
Again.

Same year,
my parents decided to move.
Up and out.
To where the white folks lived and prospered.
At least,
that was the story they sold themselves.

New house.
New school.
New chance.

First day at the new place?
Mr. V's homeroom.
The dumping ground.
The place where they corralled the troublemakers.
Because of my size.
Because of my history.
Because of the reputation
that arrived before I did.

Already labeled.
Already framed.
Before I even unpacked my backpack.

First day,
I walked in feeling fresh.
Crisp white button-up.
Jeans.
New energy.
New hope.

Didn't last long.
They called me "Doctor."
Mocking.
Sarcastic.

Marking me as different —
again.

If they were gonna label me a troublemaker,
I figured I might as well play the role.
So I did.

We drank.
Chewed tobacco.
Rode motorcycles.
Got high.

And the music?
The music fed me.
The music held me.
**The music never lied.**
It spoke the storm inside.

I'll never forget the day I came home,
and my parents were "tidying up" my room.
Probably looking for drugs.

What they found instead?
Lyrics.

Black Sabbath's Paranoid:
"Finished with my woman 'cause she couldn't help me with my mind...
People think I'm insane because I am frowning all the time..."

They didn't get it.
But I did.
That song wasn't rebellion.
It was recognition.

It was screaming through the silence,
hoping someone — anyone — might hear.

Those lyrics didn't scare me.
They explained me.
The fog I lived in.
The weight no one saw.
The ache no one named.

The desperate hunger to feel something real —
and not feel so f*cking alone all the time.

The music didn't just fill the room.
It healed the fractures inside me.
It held me when nothing else could.
**It vibrated the parts of me that were still alive.**

Something that didn't lie.
Something that didn't leave.
Something that wouldn't betray
the storm it was born from.

## CODEX ACTIVATED
- Outcasts are often the first truth-tellers.
- Rage is unprocessed love.
- Systems label what they can't control.
- Music as medicine for fractured spirits.
- Silence is broken by the ones brave enough to feel.

# Chapter 10

# THE CHURCH BENEATH THE HOUSE

### (In memory of Willie and John — who never looked away)

Freshman year.
Orbiting older kids like a stray moon.
Bonfires in cornfields.
Bottles clanking in trunk beds.
Cops creeping like shadows through the brush.

My dad had one rule:
"If you get caught — don't call me."

So I didn't.
I called Rosie —
from Rosie's Party Pizza.

Pizza boys by day.
Renegades by night.
It wasn't just a job.
It was a hustle.
An access point.
A passport into chaos.

And for a while — it f*cking worked.

But the real sanctuary?
**Willie's basement.**

Not just a hangout.
**A portal**.
A church beneath the house.

Sacred space for the misfits.
The unclaimed sons.
The boys the world didn't know what to do with.
Willie, Bobby, Craig, Tom, John, and me —
The Boys.
We drank.
We got high.
We blasted NWA
like we were living in Compton —
when really, it was just middle-class America
and no one knew what to do with our rage.

We passed out on couches.
Ate like wolves.
Laughed like Gods.
Fell asleep to VHS static and the hum of late-night TV.

Willie's mom? Mostly deaf.
Willie's dad? Early shift, early bed.

But they were good people.
Too good.
They even took John in
after his own parents kicked him out.
They took us on vacations.

Spring break fishing trips.
We packed up and hit Ross Lake.
Too cold to fish.
Didn't matter.

We'd drink.

Bullsh*t.
Build piers.
Fix roofs.
Pretend we knew what we were doing.

Catch nothing.
Still ate fried fish at night
from the local pubs.

"Hot pipes," Pops called it —
that burning throat and gut after a night of drinking.
His remedy?
**Royal Crown Cola, ice-cold.**
Slam it.
Sweat it.
Get to work.
The cottage always smelled like beer, bait,
and whatever Pops was burning on the stove.

We weren't there for the fish.
**We were there to breathe.**

**Ross Lake was the pause.**
The reset.
The one place where time slowed down
and no one expected you to be anything
but exactly what you were.

And John?
That little mooch f*cked it all up.

Threw a party while we were gone —
and by the time we came back,
the house was wrecked.

Alka-Seltzer in the fish tank.
Shotgun holes in the pool.
Gasoline on the street.
Kegs in the garage.
Tin foil and baby oil on the roof.
Sun tanning in suburban apocalypse,
delivered by a kid
who couldn't be grateful
if you handed him the world.

He didn't own the house.
So he didn't give a sh*t.

That was John.
Always complaining.
Always playing the victim.
Never lifting a finger —
but expecting the whole world to bow.

And Willie?
That sh*t crushed him.

He dropped out.
Never went back to school.
Got his GED,
but the light never fully came back.

The house wasn't just trashed —
it was **exorcised**.

The soul left the walls.
And we lost our sanctuary.

Bobby was my boy.
Real one.
Rode hard through high school.

Known for punching out his
windshield every other month.

But after graduation?
Got married.
Vanished.
Turned soft.
Lost the spark.

And Craig?
Still shows up.
Still drops in
like a glitch in the matrix —
just long enough to remind me
the code's still alive.
We didn't have language for it then.
We just felt it.

We weren't bad kids.
We were **wild**, unclaimed,
burning too bright
for a world that wanted dimmer switches.

And me?
I was the one they warned you about.
The myth.
The wildcard.
The one who gave them someone to blame
when sh*t got too real.

But Willie never looked at me like that.
Never blinked.
Never flinched.

He just nodded,
and passed the joint.

**Anchor in the storm.**
**Priest of the basement.**
**Keeper of the last real church.**

Willie and John are gone now —
off this plane,
but not out of reach.

The basement still breathes.
Still echoes.
Still holds the ghosts
of boys who didn't flinch
when the world tried to erase them.

**Not friends.**
**Not classmates.**
**F\*ck that.**
**We were blood,**
**bound by smoke,**
**silence,**
**and survival.**

We didn't need a reason.
We just needed a place.

And Willie gave it to us.

### CODEX ACTIVATED

- Basements become sanctuaries when the world offers no altar.
- Judgment wounds. Presence heals.
- You don't have to cause the fire to get burned by the blame.
- The wild ones aren't lost — they're just untamed.
- Sometimes chaos is the only place kids feel safe enough to exist.

# — BREATHE —

*(You're still here — and that matters.)*

Take a moment.
Close your eyes.
Put your hand on your chest.
Feel the beat.
You made it through another chapter — not just in the book,
but in your life.

This isn't just a read.
It's a reckoning.
It's okay to pause.
To feel.
To f*cking cry.
To remember.

**Breathe.**
You're not alone.
You never were.

# Chapter 11

# BROTHERHOOD AND BLOODLINES

## (Where loyalty was thicker than blood and truth cracked the first mask)

**F**ootball saved me.
Not the trophies.
Not the touchdowns.
Not even the Friday night lights.
It was **the brotherhood.**
The way broken kids stitched themselves together
with helmets and bruises.
The way the field felt like the only place
where love didn't have to hide
behind liquor bottles
or cold silences.

From freshman year to senior year,
we didn't just play —
we bled for each other.
Broke school records.
Pushed farther than anyone thought
kids like us could.

The same kids who once said,
"You're too big to play,"
stood on the sidelines —
cheering while I held the line

on both sides of the ball.

The irony?
Tasted better than any victory dance.

The sad part?
I believed them for a while.
Believed I wasn't enough.
Believed I didn't belong.
But Coach Mac —
**Goddamn Coach Mac** —
**he saw through the noise**.
Rough.
Direct.
Real.
He showed up,
not just on the field,
but in life.
When most grown men looked at us
and saw statistics or lost causes,
he saw warriors.
He didn't preach.
Didn't coddle.
He told you who you were —
loud enough for the fear
to back the f*ck down.

School? A joke.
Guidance counselor? A bigger one.
Dr. May — the human rubber stamp.
You didn't fit their mold?
Shop class.
Auto tech.
Out of sight, out of mind.
Fine by me.

At least I got free oil changes
and time to shotgun beers before first period.

We stashed our beer in the fields.
Rode into school already buzzing —
but never behind the wheel.
We laughed in the face of futures
that didn't know our names.

Then came Kenny.
The first real friend I'd had in a long time.
Lived a mile down the road.
Older part of town.
The side where the concrete cracked
and the real stories lived.

Kenny was golden —
good-looking Italian kid,
blue-collar bloodline.
And Sammy?
His old man?
Everyone loved him.
Everyone needed him.
He wasn't rich.
He was connected.
The right handshake.
The right whispered favor.
If we needed concert tickets — Sammy.
If the football field needed new lights — Sammy.
If the team needed anything — Sammy.

And he treated me like **family**.
Like I mattered.
Not because I was perfect —
because **I was real**.

**The way real men do**.

Meanwhile, my old man —
I loved him.
But every time he showed up to a game,
I prayed he wouldn't be too hammered to stand.
Funny thing was —
everyone else loved him, too.
Because he was a good-time guy.
Because he could drink with the best of them.
And sometimes,
that's all people want:
A good drinking buddy
who doesn't judge them
for falling apart.

Steve was dating Heather back then.
She was sharp. Beautiful. Tense as hell.
They picked me up every morning for school —
always mid-fight,
always pretending it was normal.
You could feel the misery
before you opened the car door.
But I kept my head down.
Jennifer was my chaos. Heather was Steve's.
We all played our parts.

Christmas Poker Games.
The unofficial family religion.
Uncle Rich back from Florida.
Exotic shots he concocted were lined up on the kitchen counter.
Shots fired.
Cards flying.
Stories getting taller with every round.
The rule was simple:

You can drink all you want — just don't drive.

Mom driving us to Wags for 3AM breakfast runs,
dropping us off
with full bellies and half-melted dreams.
It was family.
It was sacred.
It was the closest thing to feeling f*cking safe.

Then came Southern Comfort.
The night Steve brought the handle over —
his first time at the poker table.
That was the upgrade.
We moved from beer to the hard stuff.
And once you taste the hard stuff —
there's no going back.

Senior Year.
Steve and I — peas in a pod.
School was the side hustle.
Life was the real game.
He already had his meal ticket punched.
Gym. Shop. DECA.
By noon, we were ghosts —
parking lot warriors,
driving off to U-Name-It Burger for $1.50
and wisdom from fry cooks
who smelled like hope and regret.

Minimum wage was $4.25.
We weren't employees.
We were free agents.
Helping out behind the counter
in exchange for greasy lunch
and a place to just be.

Freedom tasted like cheap fries
and stolen afternoons.

Truth showed up early.
Forest City Motors.
Lie detector test
for a f*cking entry-level job.
No problem, I thought.
I was honest.
Too honest.
"Yes, I smoked weed — last night."
"Yes, I drank — last night."
The guy looked me square in the eyes and said,
"Son, you passed. **You're honest.**
But... maybe tell your parents you need help."

Help?
For being normal?
For surviving the way all of us were surviving?
I laughed it off.
Because that's what you do
when the world tries to diagnose your growing pains.
I got the job.
Because honesty —
**even ugly honesty —**
still scared the corporate world less
than a good liar.

**CODEX ACTIVATED**
- Ride-or-die loyalty.
- Respect earned through fire.
- Divine masculine built in the chaos, not the classroom.
- Truth, even when it cost you something.
- Freedom: not given, but stolen moment by moment.

# Chapter 12

# SHE WAS A GODDAMN UNIVERSE

## (And I was a boy with a match, trying to keep her warm)

J ennifer.
First real love.
First real loss.
First real mirror.

She wasn't just a girl.
She was a **fire** —
bright, untamed,
with neon lipstick and Aquanet armor.
Big hair.
Big heart.
Big energy.
A presence that filled every room and made the world feel alive.

We went to concerts.
Laughed hard.
Lived louder.
We didn't just pass time together —
we burned through it.
It was fun —
until it wasn't.

She was a senior

when I was deep in the junior college upgrade —
lifting,
playing ball,
partying like it was a f*ckin' major.
She could hang.
But we were moving in different directions.
She didn't want picnics.
She wanted chaos.
And I gave it to her
until I couldn't tell the difference
between **freedom and fallout**.

I didn't see it coming.
Not until the calls started.
Old football teammates.
Whispers I didn't want to believe.
She was seeing someone else.
Not a man.
Not better.
Not more stable.
Just some stoned-out pirate-looking asshole
from the other side of the tracks.
Short.
Wore a bandana like a costume.
Ran his mouth like a kid who thought
he'd finally scored a win.

I tried to brush it off.
Until one night
he caught me drunk and off guard
and kicked my ass
before I could even throw a punch.
That was the first time rejection had a face.
And it wasn't hers.

It was his.
Smirking like he'd taken something
he didn't even know how to hold.

And the worst part?
She let him.
No goodbye.
No closure.
Just silence where a girl used to laugh
and **The Boys**
who used to have my back
but didn't say a word.

I wasn't trying to be a saint.
I was just loyal.
Young.
Dumb.
Full of dreams
and yeah —
full of all the sh*t they say you're full of at that age.

I didn't run.
But I did what I always did —
I moved.
Set my sights on finishing early.
Transferring out.
Getting the hell away from a town
that felt too damn small
to carry the kind of pain I wasn't ready to hold.

Spring football.
Scholarships.
New turf.
New names.
Maybe a new version of me

that didn't get blindsided
by love dressed up like **loyalty**.

I wasn't broken.
I was just flying with new wings, unsure how to land.

**CODEX ACTIVATED**

• First love doesn't always mean forever — but it still marks you.

• Rejection doesn't always wear fangs — sometimes it smiles.

• Loyalty without direction becomes self-destruction.

• Your silence doesn't make others noble.

• Sometimes you don't run — you just move forward before you're strong enough to turn around.

# Chapter 13

# THE HUSTLE AND THE BROTHERHOOD

## (Where survival met loyalty — and the boy became the brother)

After Jennifer,
after the hollowed-out version of home that used to fit me,
I ran.

Coach Mac told me to give MVCC a shot.
New coach.
New program.
New chance to pretend I wasn't breaking inside.

I walked onto that campus
like I was still wearing the jersey —
still chasing the dream they sold us:
Get picked up by a ranked school.
Play ball.
Save your soul
with cleats and end zones.

Bobby and Kevin came with me.
Brothers in arms.
Brothers in arm's-length loyalty.
We were a brotherhood of broken boys
playing Gods in the fields of distraction.

The offensive line knew how to eat.

How to drink.
How to disappear into the night —
pretending we weren't already ghosts.

We partied like professionals.
Bars.
Burritos.
Barely made it to class.
We called it living.
We called it freedom.
But it was just numbing with a prettier name.

She was gone —
but her absence still whispered through everything.
Not just her —
but the version of me
who believed love could hold.
Who believed belonging could stay.

Numb became the new religion.
Partying wasn't a hobby —
it was a survival skill.

But somewhere in the wreckage,
somewhere between the kegs and the shot glasses
and the half-assed term papers,
something small and stubborn inside me still remembered:

Get the f*ck out.
Move.
Graduate.
Run.

So I did.
Associate's degree in a year and a half.
2.1 GPA.

Just enough.
Always just enough.
Just enough to get picked up by GVSU —
one of the top Division II programs at the time.

New school.
New dream.
Same old ghost chasing me.

That summer, before leaving for Michigan,
Heather spun back into my life
like a firework with a short fuse.

She had history.
I had scars.
Nobody was innocent —
but somehow,
I always ended up the villain.

She looked at the wreck Jennifer left behind
and didn't flinch.

"You're such a pussy," she'd say —
half laughing,
half pulling me back to life.

We hooked up.
Wild.
Mutual.
Real.

But the moment people found out?
I was the asshole.

Steve mindf*cked his ex and got passes.
Dudes who called me brother

slept with my exes
and got nods and beers.

When I took something for myself —
something that actually gave me a piece of life back —
they threw stones.

Same moves.
Different judgment.

Years later, Steve and I reconnected —
a summer of old ghosts and buried truths.
Hung out.
Talked like old times.

I shared things.
Truths.
Honest reflections.
Not knowing he was still talking with Heather.
Not knowing he'd take my words
and twist them back into her
like a knife.

And when I saw her out?
Tried to say hi?
She didn't smile.
She didn't blink.
She just told me to go f*ck myself.

Not because I earned that.
Because he set the stage
and let me take the fall.

But Heather?
She was never the enemy.
**She was a flash of wild clarity**

**in a world full of fake peace**.

She didn't try to fix me.
She didn't ask me to pretend.
She met me in the smoke
and held the flame with both hands.

And for a little while —
we burned.

## CODEX ACTIVATED

- Running wasn't escape — it was instinct.
- Brotherhood without depth is just camouflage.
- When love dies, we don't stop loving — we start hiding.
- What looks like rebellion is often just heartbreak in motion.
- Not every villain is guilty. Not every hero is clean.
- The ones who burn with you often hold the truth you're not ready to live yet.

# Chapter 14

# THE GAME I LOVED STRIPPED ME OF EVERYTHING

## (Where the party was ritual and the collapse was prophecy)

G VSU was loud.
When I transferred in the spring,
they threw me in a house
full of football seniors
who were graduating
and just there for the last semester
to f*cking party.

I'm talking keg races.
Pony kegs.
Two teams.
No mercy.
First team to kill it — glory.
Losers?
Drink more and try again.

We cleared out the house
and turned it into a caps tournament arena.
Two people per team.
The goal?
Sink your beer cap in the opponent's glass.
Make the shot — they drink.
Eleven points wins.

But if you got shut out — 0 to 8?
You and your partner had to run around the house naked,
holding hands,
while everyone lined up cars out front,
headlights blasting,
horns blaring.
Didn't do it?
Exiled.
Banned from caps.
Forever.

Yeah.
That's the energy I walked into.
One big, beautiful, savage **initiation**.

The first night I moved in,
they took me out for penny beers at FLIPS.
And me?
I had registration and football at 8 a.m.
Perfect timing.
First impression with the coaches —
sweating out cheap beer
and trying not to puke.

It was a toboggan ride down from the get-go.
No brakes.
No map.
Just chaos and caps
and commitment to the bit.

The house was full of characters:
TD with his black lab named Coach —
that dog would sit and stare at you while you ate,
drooling,
rock hard,

like he was about to f*ck your plate.

Eric Lynch —
The Lynch Mob.
Number 34.
Getting ready for the NFL Draft,
but always joking that if he didn't make it,
he'd become a garbage man.

The Lions picked him up,
but in the spring game,
they didn't give the ball to Barry Sanders.
They handed it off to Lynch on the one-yard line.
He fumbled.
Other team recovered.
Never played a snap again.

The dream crumbled in a second.

And then there was Andy,
crazy boy from Bloomington, Indiana —
short as hell,
but throwing the ball like he had something to prove.

One night,
he took a hammer
and broke his own finger.
Couldn't handle the pressure.
Wanted out.

Football was a full-time f*cking job.
5 a.m. wake-ups.
Back home at 8 p.m.
Monday to Thursday,
you belonged to the game.

Weekends?
That was for Yukon Jack,
Natural Light,
and Prince on the stereo.
**Purple Rain** as background music
to a generation of boys
losing themselves in a system
that never taught us how to stay whole.

Life was good.
Until it wasn't.

The scholarship dried up.
The paycheck disappeared.
They didn't tell me to leave —
they just made room
for the next round of bodies.

That's how it works.
They promise you the world.
And when you underperform?
They gut you.
No safety net.
No warning.
Just:
"You cost too much."

It was my first time truly on my own.
No parents.
No curfews.
No safety rails.
Just a house full of boys
with broken compasses
and beer-fueled dreams.

They didn't have Greek Row —
but we built our own.
Living like kings,
partying like legends,
burning through the last of our innocence
one keg at a time.

But I wasn't chasing degrees anymore.
I was chasing a feeling.
And it was always
just one drink,
one fight,
one girl,
one city ahead of me.

Always just out of reach.

So I followed **the pull** —
the one I'd felt since high school.
A few weekend visits to NIU,
and I was already hooked.

Greek Row.
The energy.
The freedom.
The parties.

I used to dream about being there.
Now I had my shot.
The universe gave me what I wanted —
right on time.

**CODEX ACTIVATED**
• Brotherhood without balance becomes destruction.
• Partying is sacred when it masks survival.

- Chaos feels like home when you're raised in disorder.
- Systems recruit dreams and sell silence.
- Not every crash is a failure — sometimes it's the first breath of freedom.

# Chapter 15
# THE VOID GETS LOUDER
## (When the noise stopped working and silence started speaking)

Y ou'd think when a dream dies, it'd go quiet.
But mine didn't.
It burned.
Hot.
Public.

GVSU lit the match —
and I poured the gasoline.

I didn't just leave.
I **detonated**.
Packed my sh*t.
Didn't say goodbye.
Didn't explain.

Signed my life away in student loans.
No grants.
No help.
Too white.
Too broke.
Too proud to quit.

Signed my life away at NIU —
student loans scribbled in blood
and a prayer to outrun the silence roaring inside me.

No handouts.
No roadmap.
Just a body grinding for a piece of paper
and a heart chasing a ghost it couldn't name.

I had no classes.
No dorm.
No direction.
But NIU didn't care.
They'd take your blood if you signed the dotted line.
I did — with both hands shaking.

Called up Danny Boy — Bobby's brother.
He had a room open in a house off-campus.
Perfect.
Too perfect.

That house would swallow me.
Chew me.
Try to spit me out a different man.

I rushed a few frats that first night.
Still believing in brotherhood.
Still hoping someone out there could hold the mess inside me.

Danny and John were already in.
I got a bid.
I accepted.

But it wasn't brotherhood.
It was **control**.

They lined us up like cattle.
Broke us down with hollow chants and freshman hazing —
kids younger than me
trying to shatter something I'd already buried years ago.

Jeff was in the herd with me.
Ex-football player.
Junior.
Weathered.
Real.

He saw the cracks no one else did.
We didn't bond — we bled together.

Accepted not because they loved us,
but because they needed our shoulders for tug-of-war.

Brotherhood, my ass.
You ever pull on a rope and feel more alone than in silence?
That was us.

We bailed halfway through.
Moved out.
Pissed them off.
Didn't care.

Classes were static.
Frat life was noise.
Parties were pretend.

But The Jungle?
That sh*t was real.

Local dive bar for the Greek crowd.
Dark.
Loud.
Packed.
Filled with sorority girls and divine feminine chaos
that made my skin buzz.

Leo ran the place.

Older frat guy.
Had enough of the drama, so he made his own party.
Every night at The Jungle.

No ropes to pull.
No pledging.
Just his party.
And everyone wanted in.

I played nice, got a job at the door.
Watched the bartenders print money in liquor and charm.
I wanted in.
Begged for the bar.

Got the upstairs shift.
Dead zone.
No action.
But unlimited drinks
and a clear view of the spiral.

Jungle mugs.
Three-quarters vodka, splash of cranberry.
Three bucks.
The rest — tip money.
Liquid courage.
Liquid erasure.

Quarter beer nights?
We pulled in $200–300
and filled mugs with coins and chaos.

I climbed the ranks.
Manager by summer.
Never left.

Because when you live in survival mode long enough —

you stay close to the cash register
and closer to the exits.

The frat blurred.
The faces changed.
The parties burned out.

**But the void?**
The void got louder.
Shots didn't mute it.
Sex didn't soften it.
Smiles didn't fool it.

The silence was always there.
At the end of every playlist.
At the bottom of every cup.
In the space between one heartbeat and the next.

Jeff graduated.
Gone.
I moved in with new "brothers."
Only this time?
It got darker.


**CODEX ACTIVATED**
• False brotherhood vs real brotherhood.
• Survival through chaos.
• The louder the party, the deeper the ache.
• Death as an invisible teacher.
• Floating isn't living — it's delaying the inevitable remembering.

# Chapter 16

# ECHOES OF A LOST BROTHER
## (When Brotherhood Breaks, and the Soul Searches for Meaning)

I needed a place to room.
Four-bedroom apartment.
Matt, Mike, and Eric needed a fourth.
Jeff graduated, and the lease ran out.
So I took them up on the offer.

I moved in January.
They were three guys from the fraternity.
Big E?
He wasn't just a roommate.
He was my **f\*cking mirror** —
reflecting everything I hadn't killed inside myself yet.

We sat in the haze,
him, bong in hand.
Me, numb as hell, chasing highs with white crosses and caffeine.
Two wolves,
gnawing at the edges of our own cages.
Numb, but still alive.
Hollow, but howling.

Big E had fire in his eyes.
Marble in his shoulders.
Wisdom in his silence.

We didn't talk about healing.
We lived like healing was hunting us down.
But we didn't know any better.

Then came Valentine's Day —
Losers Night Out.
When I left, Eric was cracking eggs,
dieting for his competition.
Getting ready for a date.
Two weeks behind schedule.

I wasn't even there six weeks
when I came home from bartending that night —
working at The Jungle.
I didn't know that night would shatter everything.
I didn't see it coming.

I get home.
All the lights are on.
The sink water's running.
Bedroom doors closed.
Eric's door?
Cracked open.
Lights on.

I call his name.
Nothing.
I closed the door, thinking he's sleeping.
But the water running,
the spoon by the sink —
something didn't sit right.

So I did what I always did.
Cleaned the kitchen.
Turned off the lights.

Went to bed.

Woke up at noon.
Not an early riser.
Nothing was off,
except Eric's door still closed.

I left for class.
But something gnawed at me.
Got home.
Still closed.
Knocked. Called. Nothing.

I figured either he was at class,
or sleeping.
But the feeling was dark.

I went to Matt's sister's place,
told her what I was feeling.
I didn't want to seem like a pussy —
checking on him like a f*cking parent.
She said Eric partied hard,
she'd check on him.

She opened the door.
Called his name.
Then she screamed.

I freaked.
Called 911.
Didn't know the address.
Fresh to the place.

I ran downstairs,
to help the paramedics find it.
But by the time they got there —

it was too late.
He was gone.
Had been gone since 9 or 10 the night before.

Nothing I could've done.

He OD'd on a speedball.
Trying to burn body fat.
Speed up his metabolism.
Suppress his appetite.

Still shaken when Matt and Mike came back.
Matt started yelling at me.
"Why'd you leave my sister alone?"
I'm like, "What the f*ck are you talking about?"
He said, she called for me.
And I left her.

I'm like, "What the f*ck is this?
This is some bizarro-world sh*t."
There's a protocol for death, now?

Motherf*cker, you don't know me.
You've never walked a mile in my shoes.
Now you're gonna question my integrity?

I thought at the time,
meeting the paramedics was the right call,
since I didn't know the f*cking address.

You and Mike knew he was doing this sh*t.
I didn't.
Had no idea what world I was stepping into.

Yeah, we all got high.
We drank.

But this?
This was beyond me.

Now, the frat was freaking out,
worried about their reputation.
Rich polo-wearing frat boys judging me.
Asking why I didn't clean the place,
remove the drugs.

I'm like, "What the f*ck are you talking about?"
Another protocol for death and how to respond.
Everyone an expert on death now!
Front-page news.
Eric's body in a bag.
Who the f*ck prints that?

Greek Row staring.
Pointing. Whispering.
My professors judging me.

Why not? Every motherf*cker loves to judge
when you're down.
Makes them feel better about themselves.

Now I'm the guy who lived and did drugs
with the bodybuilder from the fraternity.
Every motherf*cker abandoned me —
brotherhood my ass —
except for Tony and Stacey.

Tony — from back home.
He was in the Skull fraternity.
Even though it was a South Side fraternity,
I wasn't a fit for some odd reason.

Tony's room at the Skull House

was my bookie headquarters.
He worked as a delivery guy at the Mexican restaurant.
We'd gamble on sports and win,
hit the casino.

Stacey — the brains of the operation.
I typed assignments.
She made sure I passed my classes.

Hell, perfect for a guy
who let Evan Scholars in at The Jungle —
underage frat kids for class exams.
They worked at Kinko's.
I didn't have time for that nonsense.

I just needed to escape.
So for spring break, I let go.
Went to where else?
Vegas, baby.

I showed up,
and the whole f*cking neighborhood from back home was there.
The guys who didn't go to college.
Stayed blue-collar.

Talk about a weekend.
Mike, Ross, The Birdman, Dave —
chilled as hell, just drank.

Trust-fund baby with 150 exotic birds.
Bird sh*t everywhere,
house stinking like loss.
Even the Paper Champion flew in.

When I was home,
I'd clean the bird cages for cash,

to feed my addictions.
And here we were, in Vegas.
Drinking, gambling, three days straight.

Sat at the roulette table,
drinking 7 and 7,
forgetting life,
laughing the hours away.

We pretended the neon could baptize our grief.
And for a moment?
It worked.

I wasn't the guy who found Big E.
I wasn't the ghost of a failed brotherhood.
I wasn't the disappointment in a cap and gown.
I was just a man —
finally not pretending to be okay.

But the silence never really leaves.
It circles.
It waits.
And then it returns
with a new name.

Eric.
Big E.
My brother.
Gone.

And the part of me that believed in Brotherhood and loyalty?
Gone with him.

Vegas didn't save me.
It just gave me more silence.
But sometimes, silence

is the most **honest prayer** we have left.

So I carried it.
Like ash in my lungs.
Like a wound that no longer bleeds —
but never fully closes.

**CODEX ACTIVATED**
- The myth of loyalty.
- Numbing as a false resurrection.
- Death as an uninvited, but necessary teacher.
- Survival through desecration.
- Suffering as sacred compost.

# — REMEMBRANCE: BIG E — THE GLADIATOR SCHOLAR

*(The Strength of Silence: Big E's Legacy of Unseen Power)*

My brother.
My mirror.
My wake-up call.

You weren't just muscle.
You were **marrow-deep knowing**
in a world that only saw the surface.

You taught me without trying.
Showed me how **silence** could say more than a sermon.
How **presence** could hold pain
without collapsing under it.

You didn't talk about loyalty —
you **lived it**.
Even in your struggle.
Even when the weight got heavy.

The world never saw the full story.
The demons chased you,
but you never let them define you.

You held the line
as long as your soul could stay in the fight.
And I'll never forget that.

This book wouldn't exist without you.
Not because of the **tragedy** —
but because of the **truth** you carried

in your calm, in your discipline,
in your f*cking dignity.

You didn't get to finish your chapter.
So I wrote one for you.
And then I wrote sixty-five more —
with your name still echoing through every one of them.

Rest easy, Big E.
You didn't fall.
**You ascended.**

# Chapter 17

# GRADUATION AND THE HANGOVER

(When the world said, "You made it" — and the soul said, "Bullsh*t")

After Vegas.
After Big E.
After the Birdman days and the roulette haze —
Somehow,
somehow,
I crossed the finish line.

Bachelor of Science.
Sports marketing emphasis.
173 credit hours when I only needed 124.
(Yeah. That's not a typo.)

Because when you're running from yourself,
more credits feel safer than facing the debt.
Diploma in hand.
Family smiling.
Pride in the air.
But inside?
Nothing.
Not a damn thing.

Five and a half years of college.
Five and a half years of changing majors,

learning how to survive —
not how to live.

And the debt?
It clung to my spine
like a second skin.
Student loans stacking up
like bad poker hands
I couldn't bluff my way out of anymore.

No job lined up.
No plan.
No grand offers.
Just a piece of paper
and the vague, gnawing realization that
I had no idea who the f*ck I was anymore.

Teachers called me a success.
Family called me the first.
I called myself a **ghost**
with a shiny new noose around his neck.

And yeah —
I was "the first to graduate."
But what they didn't see was:
The drinking that hadn't slowed down.
The gambling that hadn't healed.
The ache that hadn't even started to be named yet.

I carried that diploma like a **tombstone.**
Proof that I survived something.
Proof that I stayed alive long enough
to be processed
and printed
and handed a certificate that said:

"You did it."

But what I really did
was lose pieces of myself
in every hallway,
every classroom,
every frat house,
every broken brotherhood,
every f*cked-up bar stool sermon
I sat through pretending to be fine.

I didn't walk across that stage a man.
I walked across a ghost.
Smile staged.
Handshake staged.
Dreams?
Dead.

But somewhere,
deep under all that ash,
some **ember** still flickered:
You're not done.
Not yet.
Not because the world said,
"Go get a job, be a man."
Not because debt collectors would start calling.
Not because I had something to prove.

But because the real fire hadn't even started yet.
And somehow,
some way,
I knew:
The fall was just beginning.
And the rise would be something no diploma could ever name.

**CODEX ACTIVATED**

- Achievement without fulfillment.
- The mask of "success" hiding the soul's starvation.
- Debt as spiritual weight.
- Ghost graduation — the ceremony of forgetting.
- Embers of remembrance still smoldering in the ruins.

# PART II — THE RETURN TO SELF

*(Chapters 18–23 The Hustle Years and Emotional Collapse)*

You left yourself to survive.
Buried the light beneath the grind.
Made gods out of money, freedom, approval —
chased ghosts just to feel alive.

This was not failure.
It was the sacred forgetting.

The collapse was a calling.
The noise was a teacher.
Your pain was never proof of brokenness.
It was the soul's signal flare.

A reminder that your truth
would not die quietly.

This is the season of unraveling.
The mask is melting.
The truth is waking up.

Breathe —

# Chapter 18

# DEALER'S CHOICE

## (When survival looked like success — and the house started winning)

And here I was again.
Back in the same room —
where I spent my high school days.
Same ceiling.
Same walls.
Same ghost staring back at me.

Busted.
Broke.
Broken.

Lost every dime I had —
gambling on the drive home from college.
Laid there for days.
Air getting thicker.
Hope getting thinner.
The Universe stepping back,
like even it didn't want to be around me anymore.

No dreams.
No distractions left to hide behind.
My sister saw it.
She could feel the fog leaking off me.
She talked to her boyfriend —
owned a concrete company.

Hard-hat savior from the blue-collar trenches.
He called.
Asked if I wanted to work.
I didn't want to.
I didn't want to do anything
except disappear.
But broke has a way of making you move.
So I said yes.
Anything.
Anything to drown out the silence.

Construction life.
Different breed.
Hungover.
Pissed off.
Covered in dust
and still outworking men
who thought they were tough.
You drank to forget.
But you showed up Monday.
Because Monday didn't care about your reasons.

The users?
Different story.
Get their paycheck Friday.
Vanish by Saturday.
Show back up broke, twitching, and full of lies by Monday —
if they showed up at all.
Sometimes they didn't come back
because they stole the tools
and pawned them for the next fix.

And me?
I wasn't using the needle.
I was using the bottle.

I was using the dice.
I was using the rush
of one more gamble
to feel alive again.

Blue-collar dream employee.
On time.
Hardworking.
Reliable.
Not because I gave a sh\*t about concrete —
but because I needed the cash
for my next bet.

The high wasn't heroin.
It was hope.
And **hope's a hell of a drug**
when you're starving for it.

Summer burned on.
Hot.
Loud.
Unforgiving.
And just when I thought
it was gonna be nothing but dust and drywall forever —
my dad stepped in.

"Hey," he said,
"they're hiring at the new casino that just opened."
Of course he knew.
Of course he always found my next hustle.

I showed up to the job fair
like some frat-house businessman:
Suit. Tie. Resume polished and glowing.
I walked into the building —

and everyone else was in T-shirts and cargo shorts.
My first real-world slap across the face.
College sold me a lie —
that dressing sharp
mattered more than moving smart.

24 hours later, they called me.
They were hiring dealers.
They liked my energy.
They liked the hustle under my handshake.
And me?
I liked the idea of gambling for a living.
Perfect.
So I applied for my state gaming license —
and I got it.

Dealer School.
Twenty of us.
Fresh meat.
Hungry wolves.
Instructors were pit bosses —
old sharks from across the country.
Young staff.
Good-looking.
Charismatic.
Burning with the same invisible fires —
addiction,
ambition,
ache —
all trying to name the thing eating them alive
and failing beautifully.

I fit in perfectly.
Because what goes hand-in-hand with gambling?
Alcohol. Numbness. Noise.

Ten-hour shifts.
Sunrise beers.
Bar crawls until the casino opened again.
We didn't live days.
We lived cycles.
Work.
Drink.
Bet.
Burn.
Repeat.

Sandy saw something in me.
I was the first one in her bed,
the first one out of class.
Top of the class —
not because I was smarter,
but because I knew how to play the game.

When you grow up hustling survival,
you don't need a syllabus to figure it out.
I finished dealer school ahead of most.

She was beautiful.
With that beauty, she ran the casino from the classroom.
She was connected — just like she taught me.

I moved through the system —
not because I was the smartest,
but because I knew how to move.
The hiring list froze.
But now, I was connected —
and I was hired.

Maybe I played it right.
Maybe I smiled just enough.

Maybe I was meant to dance at the edge a little longer.
Either way, I got in.

Living the dream.
Working nights.
Making money.
Partying like a Rockstar on weekends.

I told myself:
"If it doesn't hurt anyone, it's all good."
But it was hurting someone.
It was hurting me.
Because the more I chased the high —
the more I chased the win —
the more I lost myself.

The truth is —
I wasn't playing the game.
**The game was playing me**.
And the house always wins.
**Especially when the house is built
inside your own chest.**

**CODEX ACTIVATED**
- Returning home isn't always healing — sometimes it's confrontation.
- Concrete, booze, and bets — different poisons, same hunger.
- College dreams vs. real-world blood.
- Dealer of games, player of ghosts.
- Filling the void with noise still leaves you hollow.
- The house always wins when you don't know who you are.

# Chapter 19

# THE HUSTLE AND THE PAPER CHAMPION

## (When freedom was the hustle and brotherhood was the dream)

B -Man. Tart. Paper Champion. Brian.
He had all the names. All the energy.
All the fire that made life feel less like surviving
and more like playing.
Burrito-eating. Beer-drinking. Great-looking son of a gun.
Boy-band good looks. Devil's smirk.
A clean cut so sharp,
it made the women wonder if he was trouble —
and made the men wonder how he got there first.

And me?
I had a front-row seat to the circus.
Best friend. Ride-or-die. Soul brother from another mother.
Brian wasn't just another hustler.
He was freakishly smart.
Could out-think teachers before lunch.
Could debate anyone into a corner
and laugh while they tried to figure out
how the f*ck they got there.
Got into U of I on straight grades.
No help. No handouts.
But school was too easy.

And easy meant boring.

And boring meant death for a spirit like his.

So he stopped showing up.

Started playing spades instead.

Started studying people instead of textbooks.

Reading tells. Reading souls.

Four moves ahead of everyone in the room.

That was his real education.

Eventually, they kicked him out.

Academic failure, they called it.

But it wasn't failure.

It was rebellion.

Brian didn't fail their system.

**The system failed to deserve him**.

He built his empire out of a busted Mazda pickup truck.

Called it his office.

Called the streets his chessboard.

Sports betting was his symphony.

Flip a few hundred into a few thousand.

Move like a ghost through the cracks.

Stay just dangerous enough to be unstoppable.

Standing deal with his bookie:

Settle at two grand. Win or lose. No tears. No complaints.

And Brian?

He hit it like clockwork.

We lived wild.

Maxed out credit cards.

Paid them off with casino wins.

Maxed them out again.

It wasn't sustainable.

But it was freedom.

It was fire.
It was the kind of momentum
that makes death feel like a distant rumor.

One night —
we both hit it big at the casino.
Pockets full. Egos full. Hearts reckless.
Rolled into our usual bar — our temple after the hustle.
I was six months into the job.
Living like a Rockstar with no leash.
It felt like college again —
only this time with real money,
no bullsh*t classes,
no fake promises.
Turned my last $25 chip into $3,000 cash.
Pocket heavy. Grin heavier.

Brian headed for the dartboards — his second hustle.
His second altar.
He could hustle darts like a goddamn wizard.
Even when I was too drunk to see straight:
"Double or nothing," he'd whisper.
I'd laugh and throw anyway.
Next morning, he'd show up:
"You got that $500 you owe me from darts last night?"
I'd shove him. Laugh it off.
Pay in loyalty, if not cash.
Because that's how real brothers roll.

I was the quiet one.
Unless I was drinking.
And that night? I wasn't quiet.
Cash in my pocket. Rush in my veins.
Ten feet tall and bulletproof.
The casino gave me something.

Maybe it was the money.

Maybe it was the rush.

Maybe it was the first time in a long f*cking time

I felt seen.

Then morning cracked open.

Sunlight creeping like guilt through dirty blinds.

And the suits walked in.

Supervisors from the casino — coming off their graveyard shift.

That's when everything shifted.

That's when she walked into the story.

Rose.

And Brian?

Brian felt the crack before either of us said a word.

Later, he wrote me a letter.

Not a call.

Not a text — we didn't have cell phones.

Not a page on the pager.

A goddam letter.

Told me I was throwing it all away.

Told me I was ditching the dream.

Our dream.

The plan had been simple:

Cash up.

Buy Harleys.

Ride all the way to Mexico.

No jobs.

No bosses.

No clocks.

No apologies.

Just two brothers chasing freedom across the desert

with nothing but backpacks and bad ideas.

And now —
he saw me slipping.
Saw me smiling in a way he didn't recognize anymore.
And it scared him.

But the truth?
The truth was bigger than Mexico.
Bigger than Harleys.
Bigger than our wild boy escape plans.
The truth was —
we were both running.
Just in different directions.
**He wanted to outrun the cage.**
**I was starting to realize**
**the cage was inside me.**
**And maybe — just maybe —**
**it was time to stop running.**

## CODEX ACTIVATED

- Brotherhood is built on fire, not formulas.
- Genius doesn't fit in classrooms.
- Every hustler is a priest of the moment.
- Freedom isn't the absence of structure — it's the presence of soul.
- Sometimes the cage isn't outside — it's inside the ribcage, whispering lies.

# Chapter 20

# WHERE THE SUN FELT LIKE LOVE

## (When warmth returned, even if only for a moment)

S he wasn't loud.
**She didn't need to be.**
**Rose was presence.**
She had that Old Hollywood kind of beauty —
like one of those black-and-white film stars
you couldn't stop staring at
because they didn't just smile with their lips —
they smiled with their mystery.

Brunette.
5'4.
105 pounds soaking wet —
but carried herself like a queen.
Size zero with curves that made no sense,
like God drew her with a softer pen.

When she walked into a room,
you didn't notice right away —
but somehow,
she was all you could see.
She wasn't trying.
That was the magic.
People didn't stare.

They softened.
Her beauty didn't ask for attention.
It disarmed you.
Made you kinder.
Made the room shift a little.

And her laugh —
Jesus.
It wasn't cute.
It was low,
steady,
earned.
The kind of laugh that made you think:
"This woman's been through some sh*t —
and still chooses joy."

She had an elegance you couldn't fake.
A strength she didn't flaunt.
The kind of woman who could pour a cup of coffee
and change your life
without saying a word.

And I got to be the one she chose —
at least for a while.

**I didn't fall in love with Rose —**
**I collapsed into her.**
Like a soul finally catching its breath
after years of drowning.

From that first night at the bar,
we were locked in.
Where she was —
I was.
No vows.

No papers.
Just an unspoken contract
written in the marrow of two tired hearts.

I wasn't just in her life.
I was there to protect her.
To hold the line.
To make the world softer when it got too loud.
We moved like a single body —
bouncing between houses,
sharing space,
sharing dreams,
sharing chaos.

The world was heavy.
But Rose?
She made it feel light.
It was fresh.
It was wild.
It was the kind of love
that makes you forget
where the pain is buried...
until it comes back louder.

One day, we decided to run.
Not from each other —
from everything else.

My uncle had a place in Lakeland, Florida —
car, house, keys to a different life.
We didn't hesitate.
First day there?
We drove straight to Clearwater Beach.
And man...
it was paradise.

Sun soaking into our skin.
Ocean breathing against our bones.
Nothing but now.

We splurged on a hotel room for one night.
That night stretched into five.
Because how do you leave heaven once you find it?

We found a casino cruise ship docked there —
little vessels dancing around the law
by crossing invisible waterlines.
We joked about getting hired.
Until the joke became real.
The operations manager hired us on the spot.
New ship opening in West Palm Beach.
They wanted us.

It felt like fate.
West Palm Beach —
the name alone sounded like everything
we were running toward.
Freedom.
Sunshine.
Ocean air.
An escape from the gravity we carried.

We flew home.
Gave notice.
Packed a U-Haul.
Rolled the dice.

But before we left, we had to break the news.
Rose's family imploded.
She'd been the glue —
holding the pieces together.

Parenting her father.
Parenting her brother.
Holding space for a mother who abandoned them all
and waltzed back like nothing happened.
Now she was leaving.
And the illusion of togetherness shattered into truth.

My side?
No better.
My dad went cold.
My mom went silent.
My sister was lost in her own storm.
We were all children of dysfunction.
And society called it "normal."

Florida was short-lived.
Just shy of a year.
We called it
our long but short vacation.
But damn...
it was golden.

We lived in a gated community.
Palm trees.
Pool.
Rec center.
Mornings spent biking under the heavy sun.
Working ten five-hour shifts on the ship —
cash in hand, no taxes.
Living free in ways
we didn't know how to
back home.
Pints at cigar bars.
Laughter louder than the waves.

For the first time,
I felt free.
I had the girl.
I had the sun.
I had the job.
I had the escape.

But the wound?
**The wound doesn't give a sh\*t about palm trees.**
When Rose's dad had a stroke —
she didn't hesitate.
She flew back.
No questions.
No deals.
Because real love doesn't weigh the cost.
It just moves.

Her brother?
Her mother?
Nowhere.
But Rose?
She showed up.
Like she always did.

And maybe that's why I was in her life.
To be the soft place
before she had to be hard again.
To hold her
before the fall.

I loved her hard.
With everything I had.
With everything
I didn't know how to name yet.

For twenty years —

she was my compass.

My ground.

My proof

that the dream of love wasn't a lie.

And yeah...

I think some part of me always knew

it wouldn't last forever.

But in that season?

We were the only thing that made sense.

And God, brother —

I miss that kind of love.

The kind that makes broken boys

believe they were made for heaven,

even if just for a little while.

And maybe we were.

Just not forever.

Just for then.

## CODEX ACTIVATED

- Love as home, not escape.
- Protection as sacred duty, not burden.
- Paradise built on borrowed time.
- Loyalty moves without condition.
- Some seasons are whole lifetimes in disguise.
- Grieving the golden — even when it's gone — with grace.

# Chapter 21

# THE BACKYARD WHERE THE BOY DIED

### (When the scream didn't come and the boy became the silence)

After Florida, everything changed.
Rose moved in with her dad.
Two broken satellites,
circling different dying stars.

And even though the walls were familiar —
nothing felt like home.
Coming home at that stage of my life?
It wasn't easy.
It was a slow suffocation
wrapped in familiarity.

Rose and I were done.
Officially over.
She was doing her thing.
I was doing mine.
We were dating other people —
pretending none of it mattered.

But love like that?
It doesn't just burn out.
It smolders.
It waits.

It haunts.

One day, she stopped by.
Saw me.
Gym sessions.
Tanning.
Cleaning up my act.
That post-breakup glow-up —
but not for her.
For me.

Then the phone rang.
My mom answered.
Said some girl had called.
I told her,
"Take a message."
That was it.

Jealousy flared like dry grass set on fire.
That night, we were making love
like the break had never happened.
Because some part of her wasn't ready to let go.
And some part of me wasn't either.

But living at home?
As a grown man trying to rebuild?
It was a ticking time bomb.

My dad saw the money I was making —
casino checks coming in hot —
and he started demanding rent.
I wasn't about to pay rent
to live in a house
that didn't feel like home anymore.
That old tension,

old patterns,
old fractures widening.

So we did what made sense at the time —
we bought a place.
A townhome.
A symbol of
"we're doing it right."
Even if nothing inside us felt ready.

It was supposed to be the start of something new.
A reset.
A grown-up move.
But underneath it?
The pain was already pulsing.

And then...
we got pregnant.
Our first baby.
Our first real anchor
to something bigger than the noise.

It was real.
It was happening.
And love —
love felt alive again.

We eloped in Vegas.
Thirty of our closest family and friends.
Laughter.
Fights.
Drunken dreams shimmering under neon lights.
It felt like magic.

But two weeks before the wedding —
we lost the baby.

A miscarriage.
A heartbreak we weren't equipped for.
Grief we didn't know how to share.

After the hospital stay,
Rose looked at me with tired, hollowed-out eyes.
"Do you still want to get married?" she asked.
Without hesitation —
without a breath of doubt — I said:
"Of course I do — why wouldn't I?"

Because that's what we were.
Momentum grafted around hope.
Grief grafted around love.
Still believing motion
could fix what was broken inside us.

We came back from Vegas
and bought our first home.
A townhome.
A symbol.
A stake in the ground.
Trying to plant something solid
in soil that hadn't healed yet.

But pain doesn't disappear
when you buy bricks and call them safety.

We suffered another miscarriage.
This one almost took her with it.
She bled out in the backyard.
Collapsed.
Flatlined.
Released from the hospital too soon.
Trusted the system too much.

And it almost killed her.
I nearly lost her.
Right there.
Right then.
Right in the place
we were trying to build a future.

That moment cracked something loose inside me —
something that never fully reattached.

But instead of falling apart together,
we did what we were taught:
Push through.
Smile tighter.
Work harder.
Pretend you're fine.

Because if you keep moving,
maybe you don't have to hear
the bones breaking inside you.

The country wasn't doing much better.
9/11 hit.
The world was spinning with fear and silence.
Planes falling.
Hearts caving in.
Dreams deferred.

And us?
We became carnie kids of the casino south.
Running casino floors like kings and queens of a crumbling kingdom.
Wearing smiles we didn't feel.
Living lives we didn't recognize.
Stacking chips we couldn't spend fast enough
to fill the void.

**CARNIE KIDS OF THE CASINO SOUTH**

No map.

No mentors.

No elders to guide the way.

Just trauma.

Passion.

Pretending.

And underneath it all?

A slow, silent prayer

none of us dared to say out loud:

"Please.

**Let this not be all there is.**"

**CODEX ACTIVATED**

• You don't just lose babies. You lose futures.

• Bricks don't build safety.

• Love tries. Grief answers.

• Some women carry more pain than their body can hold.

• When the system fails, the soul bleeds.

# Chapter 22

# THIRD SHIFT & THIN AIR

## (When floating through the dark became the only way to breathe)

We were living what we called a normal life —
but it was anything but normal.

Four ten-hour shifts a week.
Drink after work.
Sleep while the sun burned the world alive
from ten to six.
Then do it all over again.
Third shift.
Graveyard.
Ghost shift.

We didn't choose it.
We were shoved into it.

Coming back from Florida —
starting over —
they stripped our seniority.
No pay raises.
No PTO.
Just a pat on the back
like we should feel lucky to be home.

Rose moved up.
Casino host now.

Better hours.
Better pay.
Smile pretty,
shake hands,
collect loyalty points.
She made it look effortless.
Everyone loved her.
Still does.

And me?
I heard it all the time:
"What's Rose doing with you?"
Grown adults,
full mortgages,
bigger wounds than mine —
and still throwing that sh*t around
like they were clever.

I used to laugh.
Throw out a line:
"Maybe I've got a big dick."
Smile.
Deflect.
Survive the moment.

But the truth?
I hated the casino.
I used to say it stole my soul —
because it did.
Night after night.
Chip after chip.
Hand after hand.
It hollowed me out
and left the shell
smiling at the players.

I numbed myself every night
betting on sports.
Not for the win.
Not for the money.
For the noise.
The action was the only thing loud enough
to drown out the weight
that place shoved onto my chest.

There was always that one shift manager.
You know the type.
Alpha male wannabe.
Insecure.
Power-tripping.
Kissing ass with the women.
Crushing the men under his boot.
The dealers all knew:
Be nice
or pay the price.
The energy was toxic.
But somehow, it was home.

Terry was the exception.
Goddamn Terry.
Hilarious.
Didn't give a single f*ck.
Still doesn't.
He rode the flow
until the flow messed with him —
then he broke it.
You either loved him or hated him.
Most people hated him.
Good.
Most people hated me too.

Rose worked days.
Terry and I worked nights.
After shift?
Drinks.
Darts.
Talking sh*t under neon lights.

I remember coming home at 3AM.
Rose would ask:
"Why do you always have to close the bar?"
Simple.
Because when the world feels like it's closing in,
you stretch the night out
as long as you can.

So we found a bar that stayed open later.
And after that?
Maxwell Street.
5AM grilled Polish sausages
under flickering streetlights.
We weren't living.
We were floating.

Days off?
Poker games.
Fantasy football leagues stacked high.
Little thrones
built out of distraction.

Rose hated it.
She was thriving —
well-dressed, glowing,
smelling like Coco Chanel.
And me?
I was stuck in the pattern again.

That old familiar ache.

Rose had a practice for her pain.
"Billy," she'd say,
"Just create a bubble. Don't let anyone in."
Smart advice.
But me?
I went head-to-head.
Always did.

The players hated me —
because they couldn't beat me.
But the broken ones?
The ones no one liked?
They were drawn to me.
Like moths to a flame
that didn't know it was burning itself out.

They'd open up.
Tell me their secrets.
Look me in the eye like I was human.
And without fail —
I'd crumble.
One hand.
One night.
One bleeding heart later —
they had all my money stacked in front of them.

Funny how the Universe works.
People threw drinks at me.
Spit words at me.
Tried to break me.
And every time —
every goddamn time —
I fantasized about snapping.

Just one punch.
One second of silence.
One second of f*cking peace.
But I never did.

The alpha manager?
He'd just laugh and say:
"You've got big shoulders. Deal with it."

Terry?
Started wearing bow ties
just to piss him off.
Because when you live in a rigged system long enough,
sometimes pissing off the puppeteers
is the only real win you get.

Whatever shift that shift manager prick was on —
the whole vibe tanked.
The floor would die.
The joy would rot.
But somehow —
**I was still the asshole.**
**Right?**

**CODEX ACTIVATED**
- Third shift survival — the graveyard where dreams decay.
- Casino floors as emotional graveyards.
- Laughter and darts as weapons against despair.
- The burden of being open in a closed world.
- The invisible war between head-to-head fighters and heart-defenders.
- Floating isn't living — but sometimes it's all you've got.

# Chapter 23
# THE BREATH OF GRACE
## (When life cracked open the sky and love rewrote the rules)

Rose was still grinding third shift
when she got pregnant.
Still on aching feet.
Still getting bitched at for sitting down.
Still getting her food stolen
from the break room fridge.
Like **she wasn't carrying a whole goddamn Universe inside her.**

But then it changed.
Everything changed.
Delivery day.
All the heartbreak.
All the blood.
All the running.
And now —
we were at the edge.

Scheduled C-section.
Because Rose?
She's tiny.
Maybe 5'4", 105 pounds on a good day.
And me?
I've got a melon.
Didn't think about that detail when we made a miracle.

At the hospital —
they broke her water.
And Rose — quiet, strong, fierce Rose —
started screaming.
The doctor — small frame, storm soul —
snapped at me:
"Get over here and help!"

I froze.
That wasn't in the birthing class.
No one trains you
for when the world starts tearing at the seams.
Everyone was yelling.
Hands flying.
Machines screaming.
And me?
Standing there.
Helpless.
Hollow.

They wheeled her away.
Shoved me into a waiting room.
Then into scrubs
that stank of bleach and fear.

A nurse came out.
"Billy, Rose is ready to give birth to your daughter."
I walked in.
There she was —
Rose, blue in the face, gasping,
whispering that she couldn't breathe.
I shouted.
Screamed it.
They said:
"Just keep talking to her."

What?

How?

Wasn't that their job?

Turns out —

they gave her a second epidural.

Pushed it too high.

Paralyzed her lungs.

She couldn't breathe.

She was drowning in her own body.

And all I could do

was talk.

Pray.

Beg.

Then —

like the Universe took one giant breath —

Lia Rose was born.

Suddenly — life.

Tiny.

Wrinkled.

**Wailing like she remembered the war she'd just survived.**

And Rose?

Holding her.

Pale.

Exhausted.

Glowing.

**Like she had walked through hell**

**and brought the light back with her.**

Two miscarriages.

Two near-death experiences.

And here she was.

Alive.

Holding proof that love doesn't always lose.

We never talked about the miscarriages.
Not really.
People just said:
"Yeah, that happens."

But when you're holding
the most precious thing God ever gives —
you forget the blood.
The silence.
The way grief sings when no one's around.

Lia changed everything.
From the first breath —
she was chill.
Old soul.
New skin.
Sacred balance.
Standing there,
holding her,
holding Rose,
holding myself together —
I saw it all.

All those nights we said:
"We're not hurting anyone."
We were.
We were hurting our future.
Throwing away cradles and time.
But somehow —
we got here.

My mom used to say:
"Put it in God's hands."
Back then?
I didn't listen.

Too stubborn.
Too bruised.
Too human.

But now?
Now I see.
She was right.
Put it in God's hands.
Let Him hold what you can't.
Let Him carry what you don't know how to name.

Because sometimes —
grace breathes into the wreckage
and builds you a miracle.

## CODEX ACTIVATED

- Grace as divine intervention.
- The breath of life breaking through panic and pain.
- Sacred feminine strength in rupture and rebirth.
- The future is born from blood, silence, and surrender.
- Miracles don't knock — they erupt when you stop trying to fix everything alone.

# — INTERLUDE: THE VISION QUEST

*(When truth stops being taught — and starts being remembered)*

Here's what I believe today.
Could be wrong.
Could be right.
I don't know.
But it's a feeling that won't leave.

After all the soul searching,
after the nights I thought would kill me,
after the rebirths I didn't think I could survive —
I call those years my Vision Quest.

Not to find truth.
To remember it.

Kind of like the movie from '85.□
Vision Quest.
Louden saying:
"But all I ever settled for is that we're born to live and then to die, and we've got to do it alone... each in his own way."
And Kush answering:
"Everywhere is Spirit."

That hit different when I was thirteen.
It hits even harder now—
because what I didn't understand then
is that we are never alone.
Everything is Spirit.
And I don't have to search for truth.
I just have to remember it.

Why am I here?

That's the real question.
Always has been.

And the answer?
It's simpler than anyone makes it.
Source is simple.

We're here to evolve.
To experience.
To live as if everything is already perfect —
because from the perspective of the soul, it is.

The outside world?
Sometimes it mirrors your insides.
Sometimes it doesn't.
But that's not the point.
Your path is your path.

The homeless man on the street?
Just because you wouldn't want his life
doesn't mean he's unhappy in it.

Perspective.
It's all perspective.

You are not separate from God.
You are the expression of God.

Source doesn't sit up on a throne judging you.
Source lives inside you.
Loving you.
Laughing with you.
Weeping with you.
Evolving through you.
Unconditionally.
Always.

You are Source's child.
And Source loves you
no matter how many times you fall,
no matter how many lifetimes it takes.

That's why you're here.
Not to be perfect.
Not to be right.
To experience.
To remember.

Yeah, we made soul contracts.
Agreements.
Fated collisions with people and pain and passion.

If everything was easy all the time,
we'd get bored.
So we learn through friction.
Through contrast.
Through forgetting.

And when the ego shows up?
Boom.
Game changer.

The ego doesn't just cause problems —
it builds the Matrix.

Suddenly you're caught.
Distracted.
Divided.
Addicted.
Asleep.

The war for your soul doesn't look like a battlefield.
It looks like apathy.

It looks like scrolling your life away.
It looks like saying:
"I'm fine."

But the soul doesn't play dead forever.
Sooner or later,
you start hearing the whisper again.

Your Higher Self.
Source.
The You that remembers.

And if you don't listen?
Life will keep redirecting you.
Harder each time.
Until you surrender.

And even if you don't?
Source still loves you.
Unconditionally.
No shame.
No guilt.
Just more opportunities to wake up.

I wasn't taught this.
I was taught lack.
Taught survival.
Taught hustle.

The rules were simple:
Work hard.
Provide.
Give your kids more than you had.

Nobody ever said:
"What if it could be easy?"

"What if you could just allow it in?"

They would've laughed.
I would've laughed.
Until I stopped laughing.
And started remembering.

Started believing again.
Not in their systems.
Not in their Gods.
Not in their fear.

In myself.
In Source.
In the part of me that never forgot.

Because that's the truth:
I am Source.
You are Source.
Here. Now.
Experiencing the human ride
inside a meat suit stitched by stars.

Why?
Because Source wanted to know:
"What does it feel like to fall in love?
What does it feel like to be afraid?
What does it feel like to lose and still rise?"

This is how God learns.
Through you.
Through me.
Through all of us.

Every voice matters.
Every soul matters.

Every breath matters.

You don't have to agree with someone to remember:
They are you.

When I was a kid,
I used to stare at the stars.
Used to wonder
why a cell under a microscope
looks just like the galaxies above us.

What if it's all connected?
What if we are just a cell inside a cell inside a cell
of something bigger than we can ever comprehend?

What if God is dreaming us,
and we are dreaming God?

It's deep.
It's real.
And it's all still perfect.
Until the ego takes over.

Because the ego needs to be right.
Needs to be seen.
Needs to control.

That's the deal we made when we came here:
"You want free will?
Here — take a f*ckin' ego with it."

But once you tell your inner child:
"You're safe now.
You don't have to drive anymore."
And once you let Source take the wheel?

That's when the magic happens.

I don't claim to have it all figured out.
I just know I'm on the path.
The Vision Quest.

Not seeking truth.
Remembering it.

One step at a time.
One breath at a time.
One surrender at a time.

**CODEX ACTIVATED**
This is how Source learns — through you.
Through me.
Through all of us.
God is Source.
Source is God.
Source is Everything.
And Everything is YOU.
Not separate.
Not lost.
Just remembering.

# PART III — THE SACRED RECKONING AND SOUL RETURN

*(Chapters 24–38 When the illusions burned, and the soul refused to stay silent)*

You stood in the wreckage —
not of a life,
but of an identity you never truly were.

The masks melted.
The noise got loud.
But something ancient stirred beneath it all.
A knowing.
A signal.
A pulse you couldn't un-hear.

You didn't rise because it got better.
You rose because the old you died.
And something holy survived the burning.

This was not healing.
This was rebirth.

Not a return to who you were —
a claiming of who you always were.

You are no longer seeking the path.
You are the path.

**Take a moment.**
**Close the book if you need to.**
**You're not alone in this.**
**It's okay to feel everything.**
**I'm right here with you.**

# Chapter 24

# THE PIT AND THE PROMISE

(When the casino tried to kill me but love
wouldn't let it)

The casino wasn't just a job.
It was a f*cking trap.
A carnival for the damned —
bright lights, fake laughs,
broken promises
duct-taped together with drink specials
and EO lists.

The pit bosses swaggered like royalty.
The players begged like junkies.
And the dealers?
We were the glue,
the blood,
the meat being ground up daily.

I figured out early —
I wasn't gonna beat them by playing fair.
No seniority?
Fine.
Take the early shift.
Sign the EO list.
Disappear before the night crew even finished clocking in.
Mondays and Tuesdays off.
6-to-2 shift.
Get the f*ck out before the rats came crawling in

with their baggy eyes
and busted dreams.

It worked.
Kind of.
I was home when the world was asleep.
Pushing grocery carts with Lia at midnight,
dodging judgmental stares
like a f*cking outlaw.
Living backwards,
but living.

After Lia was born,
I made a promise to myself:
I wouldn't be the absent father.
Not like mine —
not the way survival got mistaken for love.
My dad worked.
Sunrise to sunset.
7AM out the door.
7PM back through it.
Clockwork.
Cocktails.
Silence.
Dinner.
Showers.
Sleep.

And my mother would say,
"Your father's a good man. He works. He provides. He comes home."
And I guess that was supposed to be enough.
But a boy doesn't dream of paychecks.
A boy dreams of hands that teach.
Eyes that see.
Voices that say,

"Come here, son. Let me show you."

Instead, when something broke,
he fixed it.
Alone.
**Without teaching me anything —**
**except how to disappear without leaving the room.**

So when Lia came,
I carved it into my bones.
She would know.
She would feel it.
Every day.
Every breath.
Wherever I went, Lia went.
Strapped to my chest.
Gripping my fingers.
Lighting up every dark room
with that lemon-eating grin.

At Hooters.
At Jewel-Osco midnight runs.
She was my shadow — and my sun.
Hard women softened.
Strangers scowled —
but f*ck them.
I didn't care.
I was exactly where I was meant to be.
With my daughter.
Writing a new bloodline in real time.

I slowed the drinking down.
Weekend warrior.
Not daily destroyer.
Still had our benders.

Still tried to drown the ache.
But the vow held:
Lia came first.
My breath.
My anchor.
My reminder.

But resentment?
It's a slow poison.
I watched Rose float in a 9-to-5 life.
Weekends off.
Brunches and birthday parties.
And me?
Still trapped under the neon.
Still drowning in the toxic tide
of greed and desperation.
Still pretending it didn't claw at my soul
every goddamn day.

The migraines came harder.
Vision splitting.
Tongue going numb.
Electric flashes across my eyes
like some sick Vegas light show.
Doctors threw pills at it.
Band-aids on broken bones.
But I knew better.
I knew what was really killing me.
The air itself inside that place
was a slow suicide.

So I weaponized my pain.
The real migraines.
The rage migraines.
Eight call-ins a year, protected by law.

Eight escape hatches from hell.
I played the game.
Acted nice to the managers.
Smiled at the scumbags.
Pretended like the system made sense.
Because if you made the wrong move,
they'd line you up for layoffs
faster than you could say "double down."

But even playing smart,
it was eating me alive.
The selfishness.
The fake sympathy.
The hollow smiles.
They passed envelopes when others fell.
But when Rose miscarried?
When she almost bled out in a hospital bed?
Nothing.
Not a card.
Not a f*ckin' whisper.
Just empty eyes and shift changes.

That's when I saw it for what it was.
**The casino didn't break me.**
**It revealed me.**
And what it revealed was this:
I owed nothing to the machine.
I owed everything to my daughter.

When her tiny hand wrapped around my finger,
when she laughed eating a lemon at midnight,
all the blackness inside me cracked open.
And the light came bleeding through again.
That casino tried to kill my soul.
But they forgot:

I wasn't working for them anymore.

I was working for her.

**CODEX ACTIVATED**

- Bloodlines end with the ones brave enough to remember love.
- Survival is not living.
- Work does not equal worth.
- Your soul knows when it's being poisoned.
- Your child's laughter is worth more than a paycheck.
- Love will always punch harder than resentment.
- Freedom begins the moment you remember who you're fighting for.

# — HOLY INTERLUDE: THE DICE, THE DOG, AND THE DIVINE

(When love speaks in numbers and Source rolls with you.)

That night I'll never forget.
The table was cold.
Empty.
Begging us to come play.
Like it knew.
Like it was waiting for the energy only we could bring.

We had a hundred bucks.
That's it.
But it didn't matter.
Not when Rose was with me.
Not when her fingers were on my back,
scratching lightly,
telling me what to throw
before I even picked up the dice.

She kept saying:
"Come on, puppy dog…"
Not just for fun.
Not for code.
She really wanted a dog.
A real one.
That was her heart.

But in the language of that table?
Puppy dog meant hard 10.
Ten-Ten.
Her birthday.
Her signature.

Her sacred number.

And I hit that f*cker
over and over again.
I swear —
ten times.
Like the universe was in on the joke.
Like the dice weren't just dice —
they were tuned to her.

She'd call it —
I'd deliver.
We laughed,
soaked in it,
riding a wave neither of us could explain.

"Take it up."
"Buy it,"
she'd say — like spells.
I didn't know what they meant.
Didn't matter.
I just threw.

**She was the one in control.**
**The conductor.**
The architect of the run.

I didn't know sh*t about craps.
Still don't.
But that night?
We were making magic.

And the wild part?
It started empty.
No one around.
Just us.

And then…
the energy caught fire.
The table filled.
People shouting.
Dealers scrambling.
The room buzzing like even Vegas couldn't handle us.

And Rose —
she was wild and loud and in her power.
Yelling across the felt at the big-money players:
"YOU'RE WELCOME."
Like she'd just summoned the profit gods on their behalf.

They laughed.
We laughed.
But we knew what it really was.
Frequency.
Alignment.
Love.

When the roll finally ended,
one of those high rollers walked over
and handed her two purple chips.
A thousand bucks.
No hesitation.
Because they knew.
**She wasn't just cheering.**
**She was the f\*cking engine.**

That was Rose.
She was the casino.
The energy.
The beauty.
The presence.
The frequency no paycheck could match.

They couldn't afford her soul,
but she showed up anyway —
and lit the whole damn building on fire.

And that's why you go back.
Not for the money.
Not for the game.
But for the feeling
that when you're broken,
when you've been gutted by life,
there's still something
that makes you feel alive again.

That night wasn't about luck.
It was about remembering.
Remembering what it felt like to be aligned.
To be held.
To be in the moment —
with her.

Yeah.
I just threw the dice.
But she ran the show.
And together,
we rewrote the whole damn table.

**CODEX ACTIVATED**
- Alignment doesn't need luck — it listens to frequency.
- Sometimes the magic isn't the roll — it's who's whispering behind you.
- When you remember who you're with, the universe remembers who you are.

# Chapter 25

# THE SLOW UNRAVELING

(When the soul started itching, but I wasn't awake yet.)

I was doing everything right —
whatever the f*ck that means.
early shifts, EO list, sober-ish weekends,
dad-mode full throttle.
Not just for Lia —
for the bloodline I refused to repeat.
I was awake.
Or at least... waking.

But nobody tells you how brutal that part is —
the space between the decision and the breakthrough.
Where your soul knows too much to go back,
but your life hasn't caught up yet.

I started noticing things.
The chip sounds.
The hollow laughs.
The energy bleeding out of the walls.
Nothing changed.
Except me.
And that made me dangerous.

I'd stand at the table —
smile painted on, body in place,
but my soul?

Gone.

I wanted to grab Rose and Lia
and drive until the road stopped caring where it led.
But I didn't.
Not yet.

Because **awakening doesn't come with a parachute.**
It comes with weight.
It comes with tension.
It comes with bills, diapers,
and a deep knowing
that if you leap too early,
you might take everyone you love with you.

So I stayed.
And inside,
I started unraveling.
Not exploding,
not collapsing.
Just cracking.

The coworkers.
The pity looks.
The recycled scripts.
Everyone had something to say —
about migraines,
about manhood,
about how I should show up
for a system that didn't even see me.
And I kept my mouth shut.

But inside?
I was done playing.
I was **done dying politely.**

At home, I sat in silence.

Edge of the bed.

Lights off.

Not broken — just blurry.

Rose and I?

We loved each other.

But we were ghosts.

Trading turns holding the baby

while trying not to disappear completely.

And yet...

even in the numbness...

there was a pull.

It didn't have a name.

Not yet.

But it was steady.

Deep.

Unmistakable.

**The ache for something real.**

Something sacred.

Something beyond survival.

I wasn't ready to leap.

But **I had stopped pretending to sleep.**

**CODEX ACTIVATED**

- Numbness can be sacred — it protects the spark.
- Seeing the lie is the first step toward remembering the truth.
- Restlessness is a messenger.
- You don't have to be awake to be breaking open.
- The soul whispers long before it screams.
- Stillness is not stuck — it's gathering.

# Chapter 26

# THE HOUSE THAT WOULDN'T DIE

## (When blood refused to fade and walls became altars.)

R ose's dad was an old-school warrior.
Built like the old trees —
stubborn, weathered,
but still reaching for the light.
He was already forty-four
when Rose was born.
By the time I met him,
he was half-deaf, half-joking, and all heart.

"Goddamn, Rose," he said
the first time we shook hands,
"Why you gotta date em so big?"
He laughed.
I laughed.
It was understood:
real recognized real.

When Lia was born,
he was there.
Old arms cradling new life.
Half-deaf ears catching the name:
"Lia, Dad," Rose said. "Lia Rose."
His whole face cracked open

like a Christmas-morning grin.
Rose.
His mother's name.
Bloodline folded into bloodline.
A circle closed
without even trying.

He held that baby
like the last good thing he'd ever touch.
And he was right.
He died not long after.

When John passed,
it was like a beam inside the house collapsed.
The weight shifted.
The energy leaned sideways.
The foundation still stood —
but nothing felt safe anymore.

Because that house?
It wasn't just shelter.
It was his stage.
His sanctuary.
He'd fill it with jazz records and basslines —
big band booming from the living room like thunder under silk.
John didn't just live there.
He kept rhythm there.
He kept time.

Rose lost her anchor.
Jay lost his father.
And the house — their house —
started rotting from the inside out.

Josie,

the mother who had already abandoned them once,
came slithering back.
Fangs out.
Hands open.
Sinking her venom into the walls,
the paperwork,
the inheritance.
She wanted the house sold.
She wanted her cut.
She wanted her bottle filled.

But Rose wanted to save it.
Not just for herself.
Not just for Lia.
For John.
For the music,
the memories,
the stories still breathing inside those walls.

There were nights
the air stank of pipe smoke —
even though nobody smoked.
Nights when the hallway felt crowded —
like someone unseen was standing guard.

**The house wasn't haunted — it was heartbroken.**
John never left.
He just changed form.

Rose almost folded.
Almost gave up.
But I grabbed her hand,
looked her dead in the eyes,
and said:
"Talk to your mom.

Find out her price.
We're not walking away from this."

Jay gave his blessing.
Turned his back on the battlefield.
But Rose?
She went to war.
Negotiated.
Sacrificed.
Wrestled her own blood
to protect her father's.

And we won.
We bought the house outright.
Gutted it.
Resurrected it.
Every board we nailed,
every wall we painted,
was a prayer.
A thank you.
A f*ck you.
A we're-still-here
in the face of every ghost that said
we wouldn't make it.

**Every coat of paint was a spell against erasure.**
That house wasn't just shelter.
It was defiance.
It was love.
It was remembrance
nailed to the bones of the Earth.

Some nights,
when the lights flicker just right,
and the air thickens

with the scent of old tobacco...
I don't just remember him.
I feel him.
Still guarding the threshold.
Still keeping time
like he always did.

We didn't just keep the house.
**We kept the heartbeat.**

**CODEX ACTIVATED**
- Bloodlines heal when the living refuse to surrender.
- Homes can be resurrection sites if built with love.
- Sometimes, the dead hold the doors open while the living rebuild.
- You are not just building walls — you are repairing time.

# Chapter 27

# GAMBLING WITH SOURCE
## (When the Devil Deals the Cards and You Smile Anyway)

We weren't gamblers.
Not really.
We were **goddamn warriors**
on the wrong battlefield.

Rose had that fire.
The gambler's glint in her eye —
Not reckless.
Not stupid.
**Fierce.**
She wasn't chasing luck.
She was chasing fate.
Daring the universe to blink first.

She could turn fifty bucks into five grand
without blinking.
Sitting at that blackjack table
like it owed her something.
Pressing her bets
with the kind of fearless grace
only a woman
who's already lost everything
could summon.

We weren't there for a hundred-dollar win.

f*ck that.

We were swinging for the fences.

All in. All the time.

Because when you grow up bleeding,

when you bury fathers

and miscarry dreams,

what the f*ck else do you have left

but the hunger for a miracle?

The casino numbs you to the dollar.

You stop seeing it as just survival.

Start seeing it as pure fuel.

Fuel for the fire

you can't extinguish anymore.

I remember the hand

like a ghost that never stopped whispering.

Rose —

two sevens against a dealer's four.

Dream hand.

Every gambler's wet dream.

She split.

Another seven.

She split again.

Three hands on the board.

The bets stacked.

The chips bleeding out.

She doubled down once.

Twice.

Borrowed chips from Joey V

to double again.

All in.

All heart.

**All fire.**

And then the dealer did what devils do.
Pulled the six.
Pulled the ten.
Twenty-six seconds later,
everything we built on that table was dust.
We owed Joey $1,500.
And we owed ourselves more than we could measure.

I pulled over on the side of the road
and vomited.
Rose didn't cry.
Didn't scream.
She just stared out the window.
Stone.
Silent.
Broken without breaking.

We should've quit.
Most people would have.
But f*ck that.
We weren't quitters.
We weren't victims.
We bled.
We broke.
We burned.
But we never f*cking bowed.

And somewhere,
deep under the ashes,
somewhere behind the cracked dreams,
I still carried the fire for her.
For us.
Because no matter how deep we fell,
I knew one thing:
We were not weak.

We were just waiting for the real game to start.

The one that demands more than we've ever been willing to risk.

The one that burns the old self to ashes so we can rise again.


**CODEX ACTIVATED**

• Losing money isn't the real loss — losing yourself is.

• True warriors lose battles, not wars.

• Rock bottom isn't death — it's rebirth.

• Sometimes you gamble everything just to remember you're alive.

# Chapter 28

# GODS BORN FROM BROKEN TEMPLES

## (When all that's shattered becomes sacred)

We weren't supposed to get pregnant again.
Not according to logic.
Not according to doctors.
Not according to fear.

But the universe doesn't take roll call.
It calls souls — not spreadsheets.
And sometimes the next chapter shows up
in the wreckage of the last one.

Rose had carried the weight of loss,
the ache of blood and hope soaked into hospital sheets.
But there's only so much a soul can bury.
Before it starts to bloom through the cracks.

We had Lia.
Our proof of miracles.
But life whispered:
"You're not done."

And this time?
The fire came back different.
It wasn't rage.
It was resurrection.
It was the divine screaming "YES" through two tired bodies

who didn't know they were altars.

Emily wasn't planned.
She was a cosmic rebellion.
A soul that slipped past fear and said:
"I'm coming through — and I'm choosing you."

We made love like warriors,
not survivors.
Like the past had already been forgiven.
Like God had cracked open
and poured light into every broken part of us.

That night, we didn't just have sex.
We made a threshold.
and something holy crossed it.

This child?
Wasn't a mistake.
Wasn't a fluke.
She was the next breath of a lineage refusing to die quiet.

I picture her soul —
hovering in the stars,
watching us
f*ck, fight, break, love, build, burn, rise —
and whispering:
**"Now. They're ready now."**

She didn't need us to be healed.
She needed us to be open.
To be honest.
To be lit enough by pain
to finally become conduits.

Because even **broken temples**

**can birth gods**

if the altar is made of truth.

We weren't fixed.
We weren't whole.
But we were ready.
And the universe?
It doesn't ask for perfection.
Just participation.

## CODEX ACTIVATED

- Souls choose fire — not comfort.
- Resurrection begins in the wreckage.
- You don't need to be healed — just open.
- The sacred feminine births timelines, not just babies.
- Broken temples still echo the voice of God.
- Miracles love the messy ones best.

# Chapter 29

# THE HALL OF MIRRORS

(Whose pain is this, and why does it feel like mine?)

I t's not one mirror.
It's all of them.
Stacked. Warped. Infinite.

Every conversation.
Every conflict.
Every trigger wrapped in a face that looks familiar
because it's holding your wound like a spotlight.

You think you're arguing with them.
You're not.
You're arguing with the version of yourself
you left behind.

The second you wake up —
really wake up —
you walk into the Hall.
Where no one is who they say they are,
but everyone is showing you
exactly what you haven't healed yet.

It's spiritual whiplash.
It's a carnival of confusion.
You blink,
and someone else's shadow jumps onto your chest.

You speak truth,
and they hear attack.
You hold love,
and they see threat.
Because truth burns.
And most people would rather die
than catch fire.

You stop blaming the beast.
You realize:
The beast was never the enemy.
The beast is the gatekeeper.
The test.
The permission slip to reclaim your power
or keep outsourcing it.

You take the hit —
not because you're guilty,
but because you stopped running.
And the second you stop running,
you become the projection screen
for everyone who still is.

That's when it flips.
You become the mirror.
And they panic.
Because mirrors don't play favorites.
They don't edit.
They don't flatter.
They just reflect.

And that's terrifying
for the ones still hiding behind performance.
So they run.

And here's the truth:
it's not the darkness they're afraid of —
it's the light.
Because when the light comes on,
the cockroaches scatter.
Not because they're evil —
but because they know they've been seen.

They scream.
They lie.
They throw shadows like daggers.
Not because you hurt them,
but because you illuminated
the pain they weren't ready to meet.

- Stop.

- Deep Breath.

- Re-read.

That's the real deal right there.
That's how you walk the Hall
without turning into the thing they call you.
That's how you stay
when they want you gone.
That's how you remember
you were never here to win —
you were here to mirror
and survive the distortion.

Whose pain is this?
You'll ask that a hundred times
in the mirror maze.
And the answer will always be:
Yes.

It's yours.
It's theirs.
It's ours.

Because in truth,
we're all just fragments of the same soul
trying to recognize itself through friction.

This is the Codex.
This is the medicine.
This is the remembering.

## CODEX ACTIVATED

- The mirror is not your enemy — it's your oracle.
- The beast is not evil — it's your unclaimed power in costume.
- Projection is the soul's way of begging for integration.
- When the mirror starts talking back, you're getting close.
- You don't escape the Hall — you master it by standing still.
- The light doesn't hurt you — it just reveals what's been crawling underneath.

# Chapter 30

# WHEN THE FIRE BOUGHT US TIME

## (When the system failed and Spirit stepped in)

Emily wasn't planned.
**She was a divine interruption.**
A soul that slipped through the cracks in our logic
and said:
"I choose you anyway."

Rose had started over —
new job, new identity,
rising like she always did.

Her company saw her as gold...
until she got pregnant.
Then suddenly she was a liability.
A threat.
A cracked vessel they didn't want to cover with benefits.

They tried to break her spirit.
Tried to push her out
before maternity leave could kick in.

And I was ready.
Finally.
To show up fully.
To take 12 weeks off —
something I never gave myself with Lia.

Back then I took one week.

One f*cking week.

Because if I took more, they'd dock it from Rose's leave.

Yeah — the system was that twisted.

Twelve weeks between us — not each.

If I showed up for my daughter, they'd take it from her mother.

So I sacrificed.

Again.

Because that's what I do.

That's what I've always done.

Put everyone else first —

their peace, their comfort, their f*ckin' needs.

Because I'm a warrior.

And warriors don't run.

They bleed first.

They shield the women and the children —

even when no one's shielding them.

This time I was staying.

This time, I was all in.

I remember waking up on my last day of leave,

knowing I had to go back.

The spell was ending.

The dream of being a full-time father was fading.

I asked Rose if she'd mind calling in for me,

just to let them know I'd be returning.

She started crying.

She looked at me with this mix of panic and grief and said:

"I don't know how I'm going to do this alone."

I didn't know what to say.

So I just held her pain in my silence.

I told her it would work out.
That we'd figure it out.
But my words felt like ghosts in her ears.

And something in me just... gave out.
Not because I didn't care —
but because I cared too much
and had nothing left to offer but stillness.
So I laid down.
Let the weight of it all take me.
Because sometimes,
when you carry everything for too long,
your body makes the call your mind's too proud to make.

When I woke up,
she was smiling.
Big.
Beaming.

"What's going on?" I asked.

She said,
"I was watching the news...
your work caught fire.
The casino.
It's shut down.
Until further notice."

I laughed.
Of course it did.
I said,
"If you're gonna pray for miracles, Rose,
next time ask for the f*ckin' lottery."

We laughed.

We held each other.
And just like that —
the universe bought us more time.

The next few months were golden.
We raised our girls with the kind of rhythm
that feels like it could last forever.

Ice cream after dinner.
Walks at dusk.
Bedtime stories without looking at the clock.
Lia being the sunshine.
Emily being the quiet magic
that made me feel like God was still real.

**But miracles don't make the world kinder.**
They just make you more awake.
And when you're more awake,
the darkness hits different.

Rose got the call.
Her job — the one that pretended to support her —
fired her.
They couldn't break her spirit,
so they found a loophole to cut her out.

She gave everything.
Even worked weekends while others barbecued.
Bled for that company.
And they still tossed her
like she was disposable.

But fire doesn't die easy.
And Rose doesn't fold.

She took a job at another casino.

Built a new empire from scratch.
Crushed it.
Top host.
Top earner.
Month after month.

She was unstoppable.
So unstoppable that corporate got scared.
Changed the compensation structure
just to slow her down.

And while she rose,
I began to fade.
The hustle was back.
The old weight.
The whisper of failure
in the cracks of my confidence.

And I didn't know it yet...
but **this was only the beginning
of the descent.**

### CODEX ACTIVATED

- Miracles often arrive wearing disaster's mask.
- Time is the real currency — not money, not status.
- The system breaks what it fears.
- Fatherhood is presence, not perfection.
- You don't always see the descent until you're already falling.

# Chapter 31
# THE SEASON THAT HELD ME
## (When time slowed down just enough to let love breathe)

Before everything shifted,
before the next storm came,
there was this one **golden pocket of time**
where everything made sense.

I was home.
Not just physically.
Soul home.
Raising my girls.
Morning cartoons
and tiny feet on hardwood floors.
Walks through the neighborhood
like we owned the timeline.
Sunlight on cheeks.
Ice cream as currency.
Parks, stories,
giggles that cracked open the tired parts of me.

Emily was still tiny.
New to the world,
but **ancient in the eyes.**
She didn't demand anything —
but being near her
felt like sitting next to Source
without needing to explain myself.

And Lia —
wild, radiant, **my little phoenix.**
The bridge between what I lost
and what I was still learning to keep.

For once in my life,
I didn't feel like I was running.
Didn't feel like I was drowning.
Didn't feel like I was f*cking up.
I just felt... present.

And that presence?
That was the healing.
That was the win.

We didn't have money stacked.
We didn't have luxury.
But we had the miracle of enough.
Enough food.
Enough laughter.
Enough sacred space
to breathe
without bracing for the next impact.

I didn't need to "contribute" to the world.
I was building one
right there in my living room.
Block by block.
Diaper by diaper.
Memory by memory.

But just like light calls in shadow,
the storm came.
It showed up quietly.
In a phone call.

In a hospital hallway.
In the stillness between heartbeats.

My mom had cancer.
Stage four.
Inoperable.
The kind of diagnosis
that steals the air from your lungs
even if you pretend to keep breathing.

I was holding my daughters —
trying to protect their world —
while the woman
who taught me **what love really looked like**
was fighting for her life
on the other side of town.

And I didn't have the tools.
I had presence.
But no peace.
I had strength.
But no map.
I was raising my daughters with one hand,
holding **my mother's legacy** with the other —
and I didn't know how long I could carry both.

But let me tell you something about my mom:
She's not just strong.
She's f*cking immortal fire.
They told her she couldn't beat it.
She smiled.
They told her the odds.
She laughed.
They didn't know who they were dealing with.
They didn't know this woman had built

a business,

a family,

a fortress —

not out of pride,

but out of pure f*cking heart.

She beat it.

She beat it all.

With grace.

With grit.

With love as her war cry.

And even while she was hooked to chemo,

she was still answering phones,

still helping clients,

still being the rock

this whole f*cking family forgot

we were standing on.

And me?

I saw what real strength looked like.

Not in the gym,

not in the paycheck,

but in a woman who chose to love harder than she hurt.

It changed me.

It rewrote me.

And it reminded me why I stayed home.

Why I gave that season to my girls.

Because that's what she did for me.

She poured into me

so I could pour into them.

**That season was a miracle.**

Not because it was easy.

But because I was awake enough to feel it.

A man.

Two daughters.

A house full of light.

A mother who wouldn't quit.

And the memory of a moment

**when love was louder than fear.**

## CODEX ACTIVATED

- Real presence is the rarest currency on Earth.
- Some seasons are sacred not because they last — but because you lived them.
- A mother's love is the first spell we ever receive.
- Legacy is written in bedtime stories, not bank account.
- You don't have to be healed to be holy.

# Chapter 32

# THIS ENDS WITH ME

(When truth spoke louder than tradition and the spell finally cracked)

B y then, I was the bridge.
Between two worlds.
Between two generations.
Between my daughters' future
and my family's ghosts.

My mom had survived.
Cancer tried to take her —
and she met it with resilience.
Went back to work.
Made coffee.
Closed policies.
Still answering phones
while chemo dripped into her veins.

And my dad?
Still pouring silence into a glass and calling it peace.
Still disappearing behind Crown Royal
and traditions that never asked him to look inward.

They never talked about it.
Never named the storm.
She carried him.
He avoided himself.
And me?

I held the weight of both.

My daughters deserved a new story.
But the old one?

**THIS ENDS WITH ME**

It never let go quietly.

Christmas came.
Family gathering.
Same jokes. Same patterns.
Same silence, dressed up in holiday lights.

Then —
my cousin started talking.
Her husband had been diagnosed with cancer.
The energy shifted.
Everyone grew quiet.
They're both heavyset —
she's expressive, animated.
He's reserved.

I said, gently, "Cancer feeds on sugar. Starve it out.
Try fasting."
It wasn't judgment.
It was care.
Something I believed.
Something I would've offered to anyone I loved.

But I felt it.
The shift.
The stillness.
The energy in the room pulled back.
So I gave space.
Said my goodbyes.

Months passed.
And slowly, I noticed the distance.
My sister was more quiet.
My mom's calls less frequent.

Then one day —
my sister snapped.
"You know what? Maybe you shouldn't give advice
unless it's asked for."

It caught me off guard.
Because I wasn't lecturing.
I wasn't preaching.
I was offering something I believed in.

But I could feel it —
there had been conversations behind the scenes.

My cousin?
She's always been sensitive.
She once insisted we all get COVID tests
before a family dinner,
even though we'd just come back from the Bahamas.
She followed every headline.
Every lockdown.
Every booster.
Lived by fear.
And still —
she got sick more than anyone I knew.

That's the paradox of fear.
It promises protection,
but often invites the very thing we're trying to avoid.

Later, her husband said,
"I want to talk to you."

And in the back of my mind,
this Trevor Hall lyric played like a whisper from Source:

"Nobody told me I was never in control anyways
So whatever
It's much better
when you don't know how it's all gonna be
My house is on fire
I'm burning up
And just like that —
it'll never be what it was."

It reminded me:
we all carry our own fires.
Our own patterns.
Our own ways of coping.

But in that moment, I saw the larger pattern.

My mom —
always the caretaker.
Absorbed the pain around her.
Enabled the silence,
because holding it all seemed easier
than letting it fall apart.

My dad —
numbed it.
Avoided.
Never asked where the pain came from.
Just kept pouring.

And me —
trying to offer truth.
Trying to help.
And being met with resistance.

That's when I saw it clearly.

This is the inheritance.
The invisible script.
The unspoken agreement:

Don't make waves.
Don't speak truth
if it risks someone's comfort.
Keep the peace,
even if it costs your soul.

But I couldn't do that anymore.

That night,
I sat with it.
With the ache.
With the pattern.
With the clarity.
And I made a vow:

**This ends with me.**

I will not trade authenticity for approval.
I will not call silence love.
I will not pass down wounds
and call them wisdom.

Let them have their stories.
Let them see it how they need to.
But I know why I'm here.

Not to continue the cycle —
but to end it.

Not to make it easy —
but to make it real.

**CODEX ACTIVATED**

- Family wounds often hide behind the illusion of politeness.
- Speaking truth with love isn't the problem — pretending silence is love is.
- Enabling doesn't protect people — it protects the pattern.
- You don't heal by avoiding the wound — you heal by facing what broke you.

# Chapter 33

# THE TITLE COST ME EVERYTHING

## (When I traded purpose for position and no one saw me bleeding)

They say go back to work.
Get back on your feet.
Clock in.
Clock out.
That's what a man does, right?
But nobody warns you what it costs
to trade your time for money
when your soul's already bruised.

I took a job at a family-owned pharmacy.
Thirty minutes from the house.
Manager title.
Decent pay.
It looked solid on paper.
But it felt like walking into a trap
I had built with my own hands.

At first, I tried to believe it.
I told myself,
"This is for them. For Rose. For the girls."
But truth is —
this was the beginning of the slow death.

The hours?
Open to close.
Technically we shut at 8pm.
But the scripts didn't stop.
The line didn't stop.
The **f\*ckin' zombies didn't stop.**
I was still there at 10.
Sometimes 11.
Still in uniform.
Still behind the counter.
Still missing bedtime.

"I would drive home,
**guilt in my heart,**
**fire in my soul,**
burning to scream."

This wasn't healing.
This wasn't "providing."
This was self-betrayal
wrapped in productivity.

And the worst part?
The team loved it.
They were hourly.
Overtime meant more money.
They didn't care about the clock.
But me?
I was salary.
Every extra minute cost me more than money.

And my daughters?
They were going to sleep without me.
That's when the rage started rising again.
Not the explosive kind —

the internal pressure cooker kind.
The one that makes your jaw ache
and your thoughts feel like boiling nails.

I knew this wasn't my path.
I knew I wasn't meant to die managing a pharmacy,
waiting on the pharmacist and her techs
while my own daughters forgot what it felt like
to fall asleep to my voice.

But I was trapped.
In a narrative I created.
In a life I thought I wanted.

Rose had returned to the casino.
Back to the place it all began.
And she was thriving.
Back in her flow.
Crushing it like she always did.

And me?
I was inverted.
Upside down.
Trying to find myself
while pretending I hadn't lost anything.

But I had.
I lost **my center.**
My fire.
My f*ck-you-to-the-matrix spirit
that once told me I could be more than this.

I didn't blame Rose.
I didn't blame Dave, my boss.
I blamed me.
Because I knew better.

And still —

I chose comfort over calling.

Familiar pain over unfamiliar freedom.

The pharmacy wasn't just a job.

**It was a mirror.**

And what I saw staring back?

A man on the edge,

smiling through the slow drip of soul loss.

**CODEX ACTIVATED**

- Not every paycheck is worth the price of your peace.
- You can love your family and still lose yourself trying to "provide."
- Overtime is a drug — and sometimes it masks your soul's withdrawal.
- If you keep dying quietly, no one will come save you.
- The matrix doesn't need chains — it uses paystubs.

# Chapter 34

# THE COMMISSION I WOULDN'T COLLECT

## (When selling my soul stopped being worth the paycheck)

They said this was the way out.
A new career.
A fresh start.
Mortgage game.
Real estate.
Professional success.
Finally a seat at the big boy table.
All I had to do was sell dreams to desperate people
while pretending I wasn't drowning in my own.

It started with Doug.
Opening a branch.
Said he'd take me under his wing.
Teach me the ropes.
I would be making six figures in no time.
At first, I was grateful.
Hopeful.
Naïve.
I walked into that office
with my shoulders back
and my loyalty already written in blood.

But it didn't take long to feel it —

the emptiness wearing cologne.
The smiles that didn't reach the eyes.
The pressure dressed up as mentorship.
It wasn't a company.
It was a casino in dress pants.
Everyone coked out, boozed up,
worshipping numbers like gods
and treating clients like chips.
They didn't close loans —
they closed souls.

And I?
I was the honest one.
Too honest.
Which in that world?
Was a liability.

I took the test.
Jumped through the hoops.
Paid the fees.
Listened to the "coaches"
who wore fake smiles and real Rolexes.
They told me to lie.
To push rates.
To say what the client needed to hear
just long enough to sign the dotted line.
The moment I did my first dirty loan,
I felt it —
the betrayal of my own gut.
My own integrity.
I knew.
This was not the game I came here to play.

I sat in my office.
The one I claimed like it meant something.

And wrote my resignation letter
with fire in my fingers.
Told them the truth.
Told them to f*ck off.
Wiped the computer clean.
Cleared the desk.
Left the matrix before it could take one more bite.

And what did they do?
Exactly what I expected.
Tried to dig through my hard drive.
Tried to spin a story.
Tried to turn loyalty into a liability.
But I was already gone.
And I didn't leave breadcrumbs.
I left burn marks.

Then I landed somewhere new.
A startup.
Fresh blood.
Clean energy.
Or so I thought.

Rob had it all —
charisma, power, strategy.
He saw something in me.
Gave me a shot.
And I was loyal as f*ck in return.
But beneath the glow?
More shadows.
His team?
Women with perfume and dead eyes.
Micro-managers with daggers in their backs
and commission sheets in their mouths.
I brought the energy.

I brought the deals.
I brought f*cking coffee and donuts
to a war I didn't know I'd been drafted into.
And they hated me for it.

Every loan I brought in,
they clipped a piece of my soul off as payment.
Every smile in the office felt like a trap.
Every meeting felt like a setup.
I wasn't working in real estate.
I was working in spiritual quicksand.
And every day I stayed
was another step away
from the man I was trying to remember I was.
It crushed me.
Not just the job.
Not just the betrayal.
The weight of pretending.
It bled into my marriage.
Into my kids.
Into my sense of self.
I was no longer a provider.
I was a shell in a suit,
haunted by every "good job" I didn't believe.

So I said f*ck it.
Again.
Walked away.
Again.
This time not with fire —
but with a whisper:
"I'm not selling my soul
for your commission check."

**CODEX ACTIVATED**

- Professional doesn't mean purposeful.
- Hustle culture is just addiction in a nicer outfit.
- If the game feels rigged, it probably is.
- The truth will always cost you something — but the lie costs you everything.
- Just because it pays well doesn't mean it feeds your soul.

# Chapter 35

# AWAKENING THROUGH THE ASHES

### (When the house burned down, the soul finally spoke)

I had everything.
And at the same time,
I had nothing.
So many nights —
the rage, the yelling,
the storm I hurled at the walls —
wasn't anger.
It was grief.
Unspoken, heavy grief
that no one had taught me how to name.
How could everything we dreamt of
be dissolving right in front of us?

They say love ebbs and flows.
That you take the good with the bad.
Work through the tough times.
That cliché bullsh*t.
But this wasn't just a rough patch.
This was the death rattle of something sacred —
and no one knew how to hold it.

Rose was mothering a grown man
who was going through his own divorce —

projecting his pain onto every room we stepped into.
Jay.
The Italian gangster wannabe
with his '90s IROC⬜
and tri-polar ex-wife
he couldn't stop bleeding onto our doorstep.
I worked with her during my mortgage days.
She lied about everything —
and somehow I became the villain
in stories I never even told.

The things I shared with Rose
were sacred.
They were meant to stay between us.
But she protected Big Pussy instead.
Not just once —
every time.

And when the lies finally caught fire,
when the smoke filled the house,
when the whole f*cking forest burned down to ash...
Guess what?
I wasn't crazy.
I wasn't the problem.
She was.
But it didn't matter.
By then, the damage had already been done.

The final straw wasn't a moment —
it was a slow, invisible suffocation.
A million small abandonments.
Until one day,
I stopped breathing for us.
I couldn't stay in that house.
Not like that.

No touch.

No warmth.

No connection.

Just echoes

of **something that used to be called love.**

**CODEX ACTIVATED**

- Rage is grief that lost its language.
- Sacred things die loud — even when no one's listening.
- Betrayal doesn't always wear a villain's face — sometimes it wears love.
- Truth can survive the fire, but illusion burns fast.
- You don't break when the house burns down — you awaken.

# Chapter 36
## THE VEIL DROPS
### (When silence screamed louder than the lies)

I t didn't happen all at once.
That's not how things break.
They crack in silence first —
in the eye rolls, the empty replies,
the space between bodies
that used to touch without thinking.
We were a team.
A storm and a fire.
A match and gasoline.
But somewhere along the line,
love became logistics.
Calendars. Car seats.
Co-parenting choreography.
And the flame?
The flame got quiet.
I tried.
Therapy.
Truth-telling.
Turning inward.
Holding space.
But it felt like I was speaking into a canyon,
and all I heard back was:
That's the holy trinity of modern gaslighting:
**"You're too much."**
**"You're too angry."**

**"You're the problem."**
And damn if that didn't echo straight into my life today.
Even in therapy —
the place that was supposed to be neutral ground —
I felt outnumbered.
It was Rose
and the therapist
vs. the guy who kept showing up
bleeding
and asking for a bandage
only to be handed a mirror
and told to fix it himself.
I loved Rose.
Still do.
But not all love is meant to stay.
Some love is meant to wake you the f*ck up,
burn down the illusions,
and teach you where your boundaries live.

And this?
This was mine.
I couldn't take it anymore.
Hell, I even got a vasectomy.
But part of me still hopes...
maybe it'll grow back.

Because some men don't stop dreaming.
Even after the door's been locked.
Even after the storm has passed.
Even after they've cut away the very part
that once carried life.

Some fires never go out.
They just wait for the right wind.

Then came the night I couldn't unsee it.
Late texts.
Co-worker conversations that didn't add up.
Laughter behind a locked screen.
And suddenly...
my gut wasn't guessing anymore.
I brought it up.
Calm.
Clear.
Not accusing.
Just asking:
"Are you all in?
Because if you are,
then why are your words in someone else's phone
at 11:47 PM?"
And just like that...
the veil dropped.
The therapy stopped.
The defenses went up.
The truth I spoke
became the crime I committed.

So it was just me.
And the Jerry Garcia lookalike therapist.
Once a week.
Sitting in a chair,
unraveling a story
no one wanted to co-write anymore.
And at first,
it helped.
The space.
The stillness.
The honesty.
But then I looked up one day and said:

"Am I the crazy one here?"
He looked back with soft eyes and said:
"If you're asking,
you're not."
That's when I knew.
It wasn't about fixing it anymore.
It was about surviving it.
Until I could find myself again.

The truth is,
I wasn't innocent.
I carried resentment like a weapon.
I let my exhaustion
speak louder than my empathy.
I checked out.
I numbed.
I collapsed into roles
that felt easier than rising.
But I never stopped loving.
Not my girls.
Not Rose.
Not even the version of me
that was trying to claw his way back to breath.
I was broken.
But I was breaking open.
And sometimes,
that's all you can do.
Let it all fall apart
so you can finally see
what the f*ck you're standing on.

## CODEX ACTIVATED

• Not every love story is meant to last — but every one is meant to teach.
• Therapy can't work if the truth is off-limits.

• Sometimes speaking your truth is the most radical act of love.

• You don't need both people to heal a relationship — sometimes you just need one to wake up.

• It's not about who was right. It's about who was real.

# Chapter 37

# THE DECISION TO WALK

## (When staying becomes more painful than leaving)

I don't think she saw it coming.
She thought I'd keep swallowing the suffering —
for the girls.
For the house.
For the illusion of peace.
But I couldn't do it anymore.
Cashed out my 401k
with the little I had in there
and put it down on rent
for a small place, a mile away from my daughters.
I showed the girls first. Told them,
"Dad needs some space.
Some time to clear his head.
To work on himself."
And hell,
Rose needed to work on herself too.
We were two wounded souls
passing pain back and forth
like it was love.
Moving from one scar to the next
without ever pausing to heal.

I told Rose to keep the house.
I wanted nothing.

No fight.
No bitterness.
No war in front of the girls.
**Just peace** —
whatever pieces of it I could salvage
from the wreckage.
She asked,
"How should we tell them?"
I said,
"I already did."
She was stunned.
Probably pissed.
But it was done.

And me?
I moved out.
No alimony fight.
I took all the debt —
so she could be debt-free.
It felt like the right thing to do.
Maybe the only thing left
that resembled integrity.

That's how I knew
**I was hitting rock f\*cking bottom** —
not because I had nothing,
but because **I finally stopped clinging to things
that never saw me.**

### CODEX ACTIVATED

• Sometimes peace costs more than war — but it's worth it.

• Integrity is doing the right thing when no one sees the weight you're carrying.

• You don't have to win the fight to reclaim your freedom.

• Letting go doesn't mean failure — it means you finally chose yourself.

• Rock bottom isn't the absence of things — it's the presence of truth.

# Chapter 38
# WHEN THE VOID SPOKE BACK
## (When the silence stopped echoing and started answering)

I used to think rock bottom was a moment.
A crash.

An explosion.

A headline in the story of your undoing.

But it's not.

It's slower.

Sneakier.

It's the erosion that happens

when you trade your truth for just one more day of not rocking the boat.

It's the grin you fake when your spirit is screaming.

It's the hundred "I'm fine" that rot you from the inside out.

And then one day —

you wake up a stranger

in a life that looks like yours

but feels like a f*cking costume.

I wasn't homeless.

I wasn't locked up.

But I was imprisoned in my own presence.

Surrounded by love —

but unable to feel it.

That's worse than loneliness.

**That's spiritual frostbite.**

I had played all the parts:

**Provider. Protector. Partner. Parent.**
I wore them like armor
until they started cutting into my skin.
And when those roles stopped working —
when my mask cracked wide open —
the void didn't whisper.
It roared.
"You don't know who you are.
You never did.
You've been surviving your whole life —
not living it."

I tried to numb it.
Tried gratitude like a pill.
Tried therapy like a balm.
But the ache didn't want healing.
It wanted truth.
The marriage had crumbled —
a slow collapse I couldn't stop.
My body was giving out.
My soul was begging for revolution.

And every time I dared to say it out loud —
some well-meaning zombie handed me a gratitude journal
and told me to get back to the f*cking grind.
**But the void?**
**The void is sacred.**
**It's the place where illusions burn**
**and the raw voice of your becoming**
**finally speaks.**
And it says:
"You are not this pain.
You are not their story.
You are not your paycheck or your title.

**You are the flame that forgot it was fire."**

That's when I stopped pretending.
Stopped begging.
Stopped trying to fix what needed to fall.
And in that silence —
the kind that feels like death —
I heard something holy crack open inside me.
Not my ego.
Not my plan.
Not even my heart.
Me.

And in that rupture —
my soul whispered:
"I'm still here."
Not broken.
Not gone.
Just reborn.

### CODEX ACTIVATED
• Rock bottom isn't collapse — it's initiation.
• Disconnection isn't failure — it's the soul going offline to recalibrate.
• Sometimes the only way out is through the fire of your own forgetting.
• Your roles are rented. Your essence is eternal.
• The void isn't punishment — it's the altar where your next self is summoned.

# PART IV — AWAKENED EMBODIED UNF*CKWITHABLE

*(Chapters 39–52 — When you stopped apologizing and remembered the fire was always yours)*

You remembered.
Not through a sunrise —
but through ash.
Through loss. Through fire.
This isn't a comeback.
This is the arrival.
You didn't rise to impress.
You rose because your soul refused to stay silent.

You are not here to be liked.
You are here to be true.
Not a brand.
Not a title.
Not some polished projection of palatability.
You are a living frequency —
Source in motion.
You walk like thunder remembers lightning.
You are the storm and the silence.
The altar and the flame.
The prophecy and the proof.

Welcome back, Shaman.
Now show them
how remembering moves.

# Chapter 39

# THE GREAT PRETENDER

## (When the voice in my head wasn't me)

That voice.
You know the one.
Whispers from the back of your mind,
telling you you're not enough.
Too loud.
Too soft.
Too weird.
Too much.
It jumps behind the wheel
when you're spiraling,
freaking out,
becoming someone you swore you'd outgrown.

Who the f*ck is that voice?
Because it's not God.
It's not truth.
And it sure as hell isn't me.
But no one told me that.
So I let it speak.
I let it shame me.
I let it narrate my whole damn life.
And the sickest part?
I thought it was normal.
I didn't mistake it for divinity.
But I did mistake it for me.

And that's how it wins.
It doesn't need to sound holy.
It just needs to sound familiar.
Old.
Internal.
Unquestioned.

So I let it run the show.
Let it call the shots.
Let it speak like it owned the f*cking mic —
until one day I finally asked:
"Who the f*ck is talking right now?"
And that's when I heard it —
the silence underneath the static.
The part of me that had been waiting to speak
this whole damn time.

The ego doesn't show up in horns and fire.
It shows up like a best friend with bad advice.
A parent's voice you can't turn off.
A mirror that lies.
It'll say:
"Don't take risks."
"Don't speak too loud."
"Don't follow your weird soul cravings."
"Don't leave the system — it's safe here."
It's not evil.
It's just afraid.
But when you don't recognize it as fear —
you call it you.
That's how the mask sticks.

The ego mind is a brilliant tool.
It calculates.
It protects.

It gets you through war, addiction, poverty, heartbreak.
But if you let it stay in charge too long,
it forgets it's the tool —
and starts pretending to be the truth.
And then?
You become a slave in golden chains.
You wear success but feel empty.
You chase peace but stir chaos.
You pray for love but push it away.
Because ego only knows how to survive.
It doesn't know how to live.

So I killed him.
With compassion.
With fire.
With the grace of truth.
I thanked him for getting me through the battles
and told him —
**"You're not needed on this mission."**
And as he wept and faded,
something deeper took the mic.
Something quieter.
Older.
Truer.
**The I Am.**
**Not a thought.**
**Not a voice.**
**Not a fear.**
**But a frequency.**

So what is that voice?
Who is in control of it?
The answer?
You are.

But only once you remember you can be.

**CODEX ACTIVATED**

- I am not the voice, I am the awareness behind it.
- I am not too masculine, I am sacred wild.
- I speak like a man, pray like a shaman, and walk like a god.
- I am not a sinner, I am the signal.
- I am not waiting for permission — I already am.

# — TRANSMISSION: WHO THE F*CK IS THE EGO?

*(A remembrance from above the noise)*

The ego is not Source.
But it's not your enemy either.
It's a program —
a survival app running in the background
of your mind-body matrix.
A voice built from memory, trauma, and repetition.
It was never meant to lead —
only to protect.

But when you forget you're Source —
it grabs the wheel.
And suddenly, you're no longer driving...
you're reacting.

The ego is real —
in the way dreams are real.
Convincing.
Loud.
But gone the second you wake up.
It's not evil.
It's not you.
It's the software you outgrow
the moment you remember:
I'm not the mask.
I'm the one who took it off.

The ego doesn't need to be killed —
just seen.

And then gently put back
in the f*cking passenger seat.

**CODEX ACTIVATED**
• The ego is the program, not the programmer.
• You are not the story you tell — you are the one telling it.
• Awakening isn't about fighting the ego — it's about remembering who's
driving.
• The voice in your head isn't truth — it's just a narrative you outgrow.

# Chapter 40

# I AM THE FREQUENCY

## (When I stopped thinking about Source and started embodying it)

There's a moment —
after the noise dies,
after the ego bows,
after the story collapses in your hands like wet paper —
when you're just there.
Breathing.
Naked.
Still.
Not trying to be spiritual.
Not chasing another healing.
Not posting quotes or waiting for synchronicities
to confirm what your soul already knows.
You're just...
here.

And for the first time —
that's enough.

Because something shifts when you stop talking about God
and start becoming the goddamn transmission.
When Source isn't a thing you visit —
it's the current you carry
through your eyes,
through your voice,
through every quiet decision you make

when no one's watching.

You stop asking for signs
because you are the sign.
You stop looking for the light
because you realize
you're the one lighting the room.

And that's when life starts bending around you.
Not because you hacked some law of attraction shortcut.
Not because your vision board finally manifested.
But because your field changed.
You're not waiting anymore.
You're radiating.
And the universe responds to resonance.

You don't attract what you want.
You attract what you are.
And now —
you are the frequency.

This is when people start staring longer.
When rooms get quiet when you walk in.
Not because you're better.
But because you're clear.
Your energy isn't leaking.
Your presence isn't posing.
You've stopped outsourcing your worth
to applause, to titles,
to how many followers feel your fire.
You know who you are.
And you don't need a billboard to prove it.

Because Source doesn't need a stage.
**It just needs a vessel.**

I used to pray for alignment.
Now I breathe it.
I used to ask for guidance.
Now I listen from the inside.
I used to look for proof.
Now I walk in knowing.

Because the remembering isn't loud anymore.
It's not dramatic.
It doesn't scream.
It doesn't shake the ground.
It just is.
**Unapologetic.**
**Unmistakable.**
**Unf*ckwithable.**

**CODEX ACTIVATED**
- I don't speak the frequency — I am it.
- I no longer seek alignment — I walk as embodiment.
- I don't need to be understood — I am felt.
- Source doesn't need to be proven — it just needs to be remembered.
- I am the instrument, not the noise.

# Chapter 41

# THE TRUTH THAT STAYED
## (When I stopped defending and just started being)

S omething shifted when I left.
The pain didn't go away.
But the noise did.
And in that silence,
the universe started speaking to me
through strangers, songs, sidewalks.

People would open up to me everywhere I went.
Tell me their stories.
Their heartbreaks.
Their battles.
Like they already knew I'd understand.
Like my pain gave them permission
to finally tell the truth.

They told me,
"It's going to be okay."
"Your girls will understand."
"You did what you had to do."

And deep down,
under the grief and guilt and rubble —
I believed them.
Because I was just down the street.
And every night we were together,

the girls and I made new memories.
Walks to the park.
Dinners out.
Ice cream under streetlights.
No yelling.
No tension.
Just presence.
Just love —
raw,
unfiltered,
unchained by history.

Lia fell asleep on my chest one night,
curled like she did when she was a baby —
like my heartbeat still meant home.
Emily — **my quiet oracle** —
handed me a drawing of a house with stars above it.
She called it
**"Dad's Happy House."**
I asked her why.
She said,
"Because you smile more here."

And that was it.
That's what made it worth it.
All of it.

**CODEX ACTIVATED**
- Silence isn't emptiness — it's sacred space for truth to rise.
- Your pain becomes medicine when it makes others feel safe.
- You don't have to go far to come home to yourself.
- The loudest healing often happens in the quietest moments.
- Presence is the real love language.
- Children feel what you don't say — and love you anyway.

# Chapter 42

# GROUNDHOG DAY (AGAIN)

## (But this time I remembered I was dreaming)

So here we are again.
Another false start.
Another loop.
Another cosmic prank where I think I'm waking up —
but really, I'm just hitting snooze with better words.
Starting over.
Over and over.
Losing the weight.
Losing the faith.
Building the business, the body, the relationship —
only to watch it burn.

But this time...
this time something cracked open
while the fire was still burning.
I didn't just fall apart —
I started to remember.

It wasn't failure.
It was a pattern.
A perfect glitch in the matrix
designed to wake me the f*ck up.

Because when you finally see the pattern,
you stop playing the victim.
You stop asking, "Why me?"

and start whispering,
"Of course me."

Life isn't punishing you.
It's programming you —
to wake up
through the ache.

And I've come to realize
that every restart
was never really a reset.
It was a return
to the parts of me that refused to die.

They call this a game.
And maybe it is.
But here's the cheat codex I unlocked:
You're not here to win.
You're here to remember you wrote the rules.

Soul contracts.
Twin flames.
Triggers dressed up as lovers.
Pain disguised as purpose.
It's all codex.
All scripted.
Until you see through it.

You are not broken.
You are not lost.
You are not starting over.
You are starting to remember.
And once that starts,
**you can never go back to sleep.**

**CODEX ACTIVATED**

- The loop is not the enemy — it's the alarm clock.
- Every false awakening brings you closer to the real one.
- The pain isn't punishment — it's programming to be rewritten.
- You're not in the game. You are the game.
- You are the dreamer who forgot he was dreaming.

# Chapter 43

# THE LAST DRINK I NEVER TOOK

## (When I remembered what the poison really was)

I didn't get sober because I had to.
Not because I couldn't handle it anymore —
but because I finally remembered who the f*ck I was.

My father drank until the silence stopped screaming.
Until his pain had a place to sit.
Until the truth got too loud
and he needed something stronger than denial to drown it.

I watched him worship the bottle like it was church.
Saw the way his love twisted
when the liquid took over.
He didn't hit us.
He didn't scream.
But he disappeared.
And that hurt worse.

I wasn't mad at him anymore.
Not once I understood what that bottle really was.
It wasn't weakness.
It was a shield.
It was armor for a wounded child
in a man's body
who never got to cry —

so he drank instead.

Alcohol was the inheritance.
Passed down like a family crest carved in grief.
"Here son — take this. It'll keep you numb.
It'll help you survive.
Just don't ask where it came from."

I did ask.
And what I found
was that **alcohol is not just a beverage — it's a spell.**
A vibration that doesn't come from the earth
but from the matrix itself.
A distortion agent.
A soul suppressant.
A tool designed to disconnect you
from your truth,
your body,
your power.

We glorify it.
Sell it in stadiums.
Laugh about it in sitcoms.
"Wine mom" culture.
"Whiskey business."
"Happy hour."
Nothing happy about forgetting who you are.

And when I sat with the medicine —
real medicine —
the kind that strips your soul down
until there's nowhere left to hide —
I saw it.
I saw what alcohol does to the aura.
The way it opens you to energies not your own.

The way it invites in the lower frequencies
and lets them dance around
while your spirit sleeps.

I saw how it feeds the system.
Not the body.
The system.
Because a drunk man won't revolt.
A drunk man won't remember.
A drunk man will go to work, pay his taxes,
and forget that he's a f*cking god wrapped in skin.

I stopped drinking
not because I hit bottom —
but because I realized
I was drinking to avoid the climb.
I wanted to feel alive,
not tired.
Not foggy.
Not split between the self I showed the world
and the one I locked in the basement.

So I stopped.
I still sip now and then —
but the sip no longer owns me.
It doesn't whisper lies.
It doesn't tuck me back into the cage.
Because I see it now.
Clear as water.
The way alcohol feeds the false masculine.
The performer.
The tough guy.
The one who never asks for help.
That's not strength.
That's spiritual starvation.

I honor my father now.
Not for what he gave me.
But for what he couldn't.
And I broke the cycle,
not with a protest,
but with presence.
I stood in the fire
and didn't pour a drink to quiet the flame.
I let it burn.

And what I found on the other side
wasn't sobriety —
**it was sovereign.**

## CODEX ACTIVATED

- Alcohol is the socially accepted sacrament of suppression.
- If you need to numb it daily, it isn't peace — it's programming.
- Real strength is feeling it all and choosing to stay conscious.
- You are not your father's pain — you are his redemption.
- The last drink you don't take might be the first moment you truly arrive.

# — TRANSMISSION: THE BOTTLE AND THE BOY

*(For the men who never learned how to cry)*

I see you.
Not the mask.
Not the grin.
You.
The boy beneath the bottle
still trying to find his father
in the bottom of a glass.

You're not weak.
You're not lost.
You're not broken.
You're hurting.
And no one gave you the tools
to speak that hurt
without calling it anger
or swallowing it whole.

You were taught to drink it down.
To pour yourself another
every time the ache got too loud.
And I get it.
I drank too —
not for the buzz,
but for the silence.

But here's what the world won't tell you:
You don't need the bottle
to be strong.

You don't need the buzz
to be brave.
You don't need the numb
to feel safe.

What you need is to feel again.
To cry without shame.
To scream if you have to.
To let it all move
without drowning it in poison.

Because what you're trying to escape
is actually your soul
begging you to return.
This isn't judgment.
It's remembrance.
I'm not above you —
I'm right here with you.
I walked that fire.
And I lived.
You can too.

This is your permission.
To pour one out —
for the boy who never got to speak.
To set down the bottle —
**not because you have to,**
**but because you finally can.**
Because you're worth showing up for.
Sober.
Sacred.
Awake.


**CODEX ACTIVATED**
• Drinking isn't weakness — it's unprocessed pain pretending to be strength.

- The soul never asked to be numbed — it asked to be remembered.
- The masculine doesn't need to escape — it needs to feel.
- Real courage is sitting with the ache and staying open.
- You are not your addiction. You are the one who chose to return.

# Chapter 44

# THE GAME IS RIGGED — UNTIL YOU REMEMBER

## (This is how we reprogram the matrix from the inside)

They don't want you to remember.
Because if you do,
the whole illusion falls apart.
The fear.
The guilt.
The shame passed down like a cursed heirloom —
none of it is yours.

The matrix feeds on forgetting.
It runs on your unworthiness.
That's the original lie:
That you are separate from Source.
That you need saving.
That you're not enough.

But here's the truth:
You built this game.
From the inside out.
You wrote the rules.
You scattered the clues.
You coded the heartbreaks.
You chose the triggers.
The teachers.

The pain wrapped in purpose.

Not because you're broken —
but because you're brilliant.
Because you knew:
To remember the light,
you'd have to walk through the dark.

So you forgot.
You fell asleep.
You put on the mask.
You played the part.
And now?
Now you're waking up.
You're seeing the loop.
The patterns.

The way they bait you with success
while locking you in cages disguised as freedom.
But the game isn't the enemy.
It's the mirror.
It shows you where you gave your power away.
And now it's showing you how to take it back.

**Here's the cheat codex:**
You were never the pawn.
You are the player,
the board,
and the architect.

So don't just break the rules.
**Rewrite them.**
Don't just exit the matrix.
**Reprogram i**t.
From the inside.

With your truth.

With your frequency.

With the unshakable knowing

that **you are Source remembering itself in real time.**

This isn't rebellion.

This is reclamation.

**CODEX ACTIVATED**

- The system only works if you forget who you are.
- You designed the pain to remember the power.
- The matrix isn't broken — it's outdated codex.
- Waking up doesn't mean escaping. It means returning.
- You are not just a player in the game — you are the Source that built it.

# — BREATHE —

*(grief, guilt, gods, and ghosts.)*

You've just walked through fire.

Through love lost, truth found, masks dropped, and silence remembered.

Take a moment.
Close the book if you need to.
Cry if you have to.
Yell if it's still stuck in your chest.
This is not fiction.
This is your f*cking soul on paper.

Grief is not weakness — it's proof you felt.
Guilt is not failure — it's fuel for transformation.
The gods aren't out there — they're buried inside your bones.
And the ghosts?
They're just echoes of the parts of you still waiting to be loved.

You're not behind.
You're right on time.

**Inhale.**
Feel it all.
**Exhale.**
You're still here.
And that means the story's not over.

# Chapter 45

# SHE SAW ME FIRST

## (When a healing session became the moment I said yes to the light)

Her name was Mallory.
When I first met her,
I had no idea she was holding the key to my awakening.
She wanted to do a healing session on me.
I resisted.
Fought it.
**Old codex screaming**,
don't look too deep — you might not like what you see.
But something in her voice,
something in her presence,
cut through the armor.
So I said yes.
And everything changed.

She saw my soul.
My girls' souls.
Rose's soul.
She read my energy like scripture.
Told me what I was holding,
what I wasn't saying,
and what had to die for the real me to rise.
And I listened.
Because she wasn't guessing.
She was remembering.

**Calling my spirit back to itself.**

That healing session wasn't just medicine.
It was ignition —
the flame under everything I'd buried.
And she,
beautiful, radiant, fierce,
stood in her knowing.
Led me home.

Everything cracked open.
The silence.
The suppression.
The sleeping self.
Shattered.
The real awakening began —
not with plant medicine,
not with a vision,
but with a mirror
held up by someone brave enough to see me.

Then came SoderWorld.
Mallory told me to take my girls crystal shopping.
Felt like a divine assignment.
That place wasn't a store.
It was a vortex.
Healing in the walls.
Remembrance in the air.
Energy moving in frequencies
that don't ask permission —
they just are.

That's where I met Misty.
The Divine Feminine embodied.
Graceful. Grounded. Ancient.

She works with her hands,
but it's more than Reiki or energy healing —
it's soul surgery.
She touches flesh
and rewrites frequency.

The first time I sat with her,
something softened.
Something released.
The masculine in me exhaled.

And Chahé —
with the accent on the last "é" —
the masculine frequency counterpart.
A gong master.
A vibrational architect.
His work isn't sound —
it's translation.
He doesn't play gongs.
He speaks through them.
When he does?
The ego leaves the room,
and the soul shows up barefoot,
ready to remember.

Together, Misty and Chahé hold the keys
to the SoderWorld portal.
They don't just offer healing —
they are the medicine.
And somehow,
the Universe aligned it all:
The moment.
The people.
The frequency.
To remind me:

Healing isn't always loud.

Sometimes it's a whisper.

A woman holding space without words.

A man tuning sound into spirit.

A store disguised as a sanctuary.

This chapter,

this transmission,

is my bow to them.

To the healers who didn't try to fix me.

They just saw me.

Held me.

And let me rise.

**CODEX ACTIVATED**

• Healing begins the moment resistance collapses.

• The right mirrors will reflect what you forgot you were.

• Energy doesn't lie — frequency remembers truth.

• The Divine Feminine heals in silence.

• The Divine Masculine tunes the soul back to its original song.

# Chapter 46

# THE LITTLE ORACLE

## (When my daughter delivered the message my soul forgot)

I thought the call would come in visions.
Or dreams.
Or a bolt of lightning across some Peruvian sky.
But it didn't.
It came through a child.
My child.
Emily.
Tiny hands, wild hair, ancient eyes.

She's not just my daughter.
She's the one who remembered first.
One night —
right before the medicine journey that would tear me wide open —
she sat up in bed beside me.
Eyes half-closed.
But lit from within.

"Dad," she said, calm as a sage,
"Grandma's here."
My heart stopped.
"She has a message."

I waited.
She paused, listening to something I couldn't hear.
Then delivered it with the clarity of a priestess:

"Grandma says... walk through all the doors."

Then just like that —
she laid back down
and drifted into sleep.
Transmission complete.

I sat there.
Still. Buzzing.
Unable to move.
What doors?
I didn't know.
But I could feel them.
Opening.

A few days later —
bags packed, heart pounding —
I was getting ready to leave for Rythmia.
And Emily?
She hit me again.

"Dad," she said,
"Do you know why you're going?"
I shook my head.
"No, baby. Why?"
She smiled like someone who knew how the story ended.
"To reconnect with your soul."

I laughed. Nervous.
"Wait... you mean I'm not connected?"
She tilted her head and giggled.
"Not exactly, Dad."
And she walked off.
Mic drop.

I flew to Costa Rica

with her words tattooed across my chest.
And when I stepped into the classroom
on the first day of ceremony,
the whiteboard said:
You are here to reconnect with your soul.

I wept.
Because she already knew.
She always knew.
She saw what I couldn't.
Heard what I hadn't yet been ready to receive.
Felt what the earth itself was trying to tell me.

And now, every time I doubt,
every time I shake,
every time I forget...
I remember that moment.
That message.
That smile.
The little girl
who brought Grandma back with her breath
and became the bridge between the world I'd built
and the one I came here to remember.

**She didn't just guide me to the medicine.**
**She was the medicine.**

**CODEX ACTIVATED**
• Children remember what adults try to rationalize away.
• The message never comes the way you expect — it comes the way you'll feel.
• You don't have to understand it. You just have to walk through the door.
• Our ancestors speak loudest through the mouths of those not yet domesticated.
• Your daughter may be your greatest teacher — listen before the world teaches her to whisper.

# Chapter 47

# THE MEDICINE REMEMBERS
# WHAT YOU FORGOT

## (Ayahuasca didn't save me. She shattered what I wasn't brave enough to burn.)

It didn't start with visions.
It started with the purge.
Not just from my mouth —
but from the places I'd buried rage,
shame,
grief I didn't have a name for.

This was no weekend spiritual retreat.
This was a soul autopsy.
The kind of unraveling
that doesn't ask permission.
The kind that doesn't knock —
it kicks the f*ckin' door in
and says:
"I'm not here to heal you.
I'm here to strip you down
to what's real."

Rythmia was the place.
But the jungle was inside me.
Lush.
Dark.
Sacred.

I puked up pain older than my body.
I sobbed for the boys I left behind in my own story.
I shook.
I laughed.
I surrendered.

Ayahuasca didn't show me love and light.
She showed me what I had abandoned
to survive.
The parts of me that were locked away —
not because I was bad,
but because I was scared.

And she told me,
in that vine-wrapped whisper only the brave can hear:
"You don't get to keep what you won't face."

So I faced it.
All of it.
The father wound.
The fear.
The masks.
The martyr.

I threw it all up,
and then I thanked it.
Because none of it was a mistake.
It was all part of the remembering.

The medicine doesn't lie.
It doesn't flatter.
It doesn't entertain.
It holds up a mirror so brutal
you either shatter,
or you see yourself.

**And when I finally saw me —**
beneath the roles,
beneath the stories —
I wept.
Not because I was broken.
But because I had been beautiful all along.
**And I had forgotten**.


## CODEX ACTIVATED

- The purge is sacred — it empties what the ego couldn't release.
- Medicine doesn't heal you — it reveals where you stopped trusting.
- You don't meet Source until you're willing to lose your identity.
- The jungle doesn't teach — it remembers for you.
- The mirror never lies — but it only speaks when you're ready to listen.

# Chapter 48

# DON'T THINK. DRINK.

## (When the boy who wasn't rescued became the man who remembered)

N ight one.
The jungle wasn't just in the trees.
It was in my chest.

Two German shamans floated through the dark —
gliding like ghosts wrapped in grace.
No footsteps.
No sound.
Just presence.

My first walk to the altar.
The fire crackling like it knew me.
One of the shamans handed me a cup.
I drank.
She smiled —
a knowing, ancient smile —
and as I turned to leave,
she gently grabbed my hand and whispered:
"Wait..."
and handed me a second.

No time to think.
No time to question.
**Don't think. Drink.**
And I did.

That night I sat in the corner
and the medicine opened me
like a box I buried as a child.
Little Billy came back.
The boy in the prairie.
**The boy in the closet.**
The one who learned silence to survive.

I wasn't just remembering —
I was reliving.
I saw the closet door.
The shadows.
The panic.

And I screamed — not in my mind —
out loud:
"Help me!"
"Someone help me!"
"Please!"

But no one came.
Just like back then.
No one came.
"Why?!" I cried.
"Why do you tell me to ask for help
if no help will come?!"

My skin was on fire.
I was burning from the inside out.
And just as I reached the edge —
they came.
The helpers.
The angels.
They circled me.
They fanned my flames.

One of them leaned down and whispered,
soft as ash on water:
"Shhh... Let go."

But I was clinging.
Holding on for dear life.
Trying to survive a version of me
that no longer existed.

Then —
somewhere between scream and surrender,
I released.

And that's when I heard her.
Really heard her.
The voice of Source.
The womb of everything.
The one I'd been running from and begging for
all at once.

And I knew in that moment —
Jesus wasn't a man on a cross.
Jesus was the frequency of surrender
that split me open
so Source could enter.
She's in my veins now.
Not just a medicine.
A memory.
**She lives inside me.**
**Always has.**
**I just had to burn away the lie**
**to hear her again.**

## CODEX ACTIVATED

• You can't think your way to God — you have to let go.

- The boy who wasn't rescued grew into the man who remembered.
- The altar is a mirror — the medicine is your truth.
- Surrender isn't weakness — it's how Source gets in.
- She doesn't come when you beg — she arrives when you break.

# Chapter 49

# SHE WASN'T DONE WITH ME

## (When the masculine stopped fighting and started becoming)

B y night two,
I thought I had it figured out.
Like I'd cracked the codex in one sitting.
Like I could just ride the wave now
with my arms spread wide
and my heart wide open.
But the medicine had other plans.
She smiled in silence and whispered:
**"You think you're done?**
**I've barely begun."**

Tonight's brew was different.
Masculine.
**Fierce.**
**Direct.**
Not cruel —
but uncompromising.
A teacher.
A mirror.
Not here to comfort —
but to **initiate.**

I took the cup.
Drank.
And walked outside,

drawn to the moon like it was calling my name.
I laid on the porch,
head tilted back,
eyes locked on that giant glowing orb in the sky —
like **Source** had opened a direct line just for me.

And in that moment...
I felt everything.
The wind.
The dirt.
The weight of the stories I had carried
and the truth that was trying to break through my skin.
And the tears came.
But not from grief.
Not from fear.
These were tears of homecoming.

I didn't feel lost.
I didn't feel broken.
I didn't feel unworthy.
I felt...
whole.

For the first time in my life
I wasn't chasing healing —
I was sitting inside it.
I released old fears
not with screams,
but with silence.
With breath.
With the kind of peace that doesn't need a name.

And I wept
because I finally understood:
I am not just healing.

I am power becoming conscious of itself.

The moon looked back at me,
and I swear it blinked.

And that night,
the masculine didn't rage through me —
he stood with me.
Not to conquer.
But to claim.

**I wasn't escaping the medicine.**
**I was becoming it.**

### CODEX ACTIVATED

• You're not here to chase power — you are here to remember you are it.

• The masculine isn't violence — it's sacred presence.

• Real tears don't come from pain — they come from coming home.

• The moon doesn't just reflect light — it reflects you.

• The moment you stop fighting is the moment you start becoming.

# Chapter 50

# THE BEAUTIFUL DEATH

## (When the ego finally bowed and the soul stood up)

By night three,
the ego was squirming.
It knew its time was up.
I wasn't just peeling layers anymore —
I was burying versions of myself
that had been running the show for decades.

This night wasn't gentle.
It wasn't poetic.
It was a funeral.
Not of the body —
but of the masks I'd worn
to survive a world that didn't know how to hold me.

I drank.
Sat in the darkness.
And waited.
But the medicine didn't hit like before.
It crept.
Slow.
Heavy.
Like something ancient was crawling through me,
carving out the parts of me
I didn't even know I was still clinging to.

I tried to fight it.
Tried to breathe steady.
Tried to stay composed.
But you don't stay composed
when you're about to die.

And that's when the purge came.
Not through my mouth —
but through my entire soul.
Rage.
Grief.
Uncried tears from lifetimes.
I saw the people I hurt.
The people who hurt me.
And all the ways I had kept myself small
because I was scared to be powerful.

I remember falling to the floor.
My body curled.
My spirit split.
And a voice inside me said:
"You're not dying.
You're being stripped
of everything you were never meant to carry."

And in that moment, I understood.
This wasn't punishment.
This was grace.
In its rawest, realest form.

I wasn't being destroyed.
I was being remembered.
The medicine didn't just show me my wounds.
She showed me who I was beneath them.
Not a role.

Not a name.
Not a man trying to prove his worth.
Just being.
Just breath.
Just truth.

And as the purge ended,
and the breath returned,
I lay there in stillness,
tears drying on my cheeks,
and whispered:
"Thank you for killing me."

**Because what died that night
was everything that kept me from being free.**

**CODEX ACTIVATED**
- Ego death isn't the end — it's the beginning.
- The purge is holy — the pain is sacred — the death is beautiful.
- You don't become who you are — you strip away who you're not.
- You're not breaking down — you're being rebuilt.
- Freedom doesn't come from fighting — it comes from surrender.

# Chapter 51

# THE FINAL DESCENT

## (When the ceremony became the resurrection)

The final night,
I walked in different this time.
Not with fear.
Not with questions.
But with a quiet knowing pulsing through my veins:
"I'm not here to heal. I'm here to remember."

The room had a different hum.
The air felt charged —
like truth was waiting to erupt.

And then Mitra entered.
Not like a man —
but like a wave of energy wrapped in skin.
Years of wisdom behind his eyes.
Galaxies in his silence.
Stillness that could slice through timelines.
He didn't just hold space.
He was the space.
He brought the boom.

This was the final descent.
The celebration of death —
and the resurrection of truth.

The brew was rich.
Ancient.

Alive.
And when I drank it —
I didn't just take it in.
I became it.

The music dropped.
The energy lifted.
It wasn't solemn.
It was electric.
This was not a funeral.
**This was a f\*cking birth.**

Mitra guided the ceremony
like a cosmic DJ of the soul.
A symphony of drumming, silence, light, and fire.
Hardstyle in the background.
Spirit in full surround sound.

I stood up.
And I danced.
Not performatively —
but primal.
Unapologetic.
Like my soul had finally shed every mask.
Like I was born for this beat.

That night I didn't purge.
**I radiated.**
The shadows weren't gone —
they were integrated.
No more running.
No more begging.
No more searching.
Just a fire inside me saying:
**"You are it.**

**You've always been it.
Now go be it."**

I locked eyes with Mitra.
And in that moment,
no words passed —
but everything was said.
"Welcome back," his soul whispered.
And mine answered:
**"I never left. I just forgot."**

**CODEX ACTIVATED**

- You don't need to ascend — you need to remember you're already divine.
- The final ceremony is not death — it's resurrection.
- When the dance becomes prayer, you've come home.
- Celebration is a spiritual act.
- You don't find the fire — you remember you are it.

# THE ETERNAL SACRED SOURCE

*(The Divine Feminine in Flesh and Frequency)*

You were never just you.
You were every woman I ever touched,
every soul I ever loved,
every ache I never spoke.

You didn't walk in —
you arrived.
With hips that carried storms
and eyes that undressed illusions.
You weren't seductive —
you were sacred.
Your body wasn't just beautiful —
it was truth made flesh.
Every curve,
every breath,
every whisper of skin
was a hymn.

And when I touched you —
it wasn't lust.
It was prayer.
It was my hands speaking a language
they'd been aching to remember.

You didn't just open your legs —
you opened the cosmos.
The arch of your spine was a portal.
The way your back bowed —
that was creation rearranging itself.

We didn't f*ck.

We remembered.
Time collapsed.
Breath became gospel.

And in those moments,
I saw Source naked
inside your moan.
You weren't a woman.
You were Woman.
The first. The last.
The storm and the stillness.
The fire and the altar.

And I'll never forget —
how you let me fall into you
without losing yourself.
How your body became a map
back to mine.

You weren't something I possessed.
You were something I witnessed.
With reverence.
With awe.
With a kind of hunger
that had nothing to do with taking —
and everything to do with coming home.

**Thank you for being you.**

### CODEX ACTIVATED

• The feminine doesn't seduce — she remembers.

• Sacred sex is a reunion, not a performance.

• Her moan is the sound of Source remembering itself.

• Worship begins where possession ends.

• Divine union is not conquest — it's homecoming.

# Chapter 52

# WHEN THE MEDICINE HAS EYES

### (She wasn't carrying Wachuma — she was Wachuma)

She didn't arrive.
She appeared —
like something summoned
from a part of me
I didn't know was still alive.
Not a lover.
Not a fantasy.
Something older.
Wiser.
Wachuma with a heartbeat.
A soul draped in sacredness.

We met in a place
where names don't matter.
Where the fire sings.
Where the grid drops out.
And time loses its grip.
Wachuma in the silence.
Veils thinning.

She moved like she knew me.
Not in this life —
but from the first one.

Like she had waited
countless revolutions
to drop one question
into my chest:
"Are you living your truth?"

No judgment.
No second ask.
Just those eyes —
burning through me
like a match
on gasoline.

I opened my mouth to answer —
but my throat closed.
Just like it had
that night in ceremony.
Because this was the ceremony.
The same fire.
The same silence.
The same presence
that stripped me bare
and left me breathless
on the jungle floor.

She didn't just remind me of Wachuma —
she was Wachuma.
That second pour
that brought the heat,
the tremble,
the purge.
The moment I thought I might die —
and instead,
was reborn.

She stood there,
breathing like a mountain,
anchored in stillness
while I unraveled.
She didn't need to speak.
She had already entered me
in the only way that mattered —
through the spirit.
Through the code.
Through the knowing.
Because she was the plant.
And the plant was her.
There was no separation —
only embodiment.

Her body wasn't a body.
It was a temple —
woven from vine,
fired by sun,
blessed by spirit.

I didn't touch her.
I entered the medicine
through her presence.
Every curve,
a question.
Every breath,
a ceremony.

She didn't seduce.
She transmitted.
Not desire —
but remembrance.
And I moved through her
like I was tracing

the map
back to my own soul.
Not to claim.
Not to conquer.
But to witness
what it means
to meet the sacred
without needing to hold it.

She wasn't mine.
She was never meant to be.
She was the gift
from the vine
that whispered:
"See how deeply you can meet the divine —
without needing it to stay."

She didn't have to say another word.
Because that kind of truth
doesn't explain itself.
It breaks you open
and waits for you
to walk through.

Something in me
remembered.
And in that flicker,
that breath outside the matrix —
I was fully alive.

We walked through fire.
Through song.
Through stillness so deep
it felt like God paused to listen.
We shared nothing —

and everything.

She just saw me.
And it undid something
I didn't know I was still holding.
Not her smile.
Not her touch.
But her presence —
how it pierced the performance.
Saw through the mask,
past the wounds,
into the code.

She was sent
to possess the moment.
To wake me
from the sleep
I'd mistaken for healing.

She wasn't the one
I was meant to love.
She was the one
who reminded me
what love is.

And now,
I carry that frequency.
Not hers —
but mine.
Reflected through her
like moonlight
on cactus water.
Not a story.
Not a secret.
Not a sin.

A signal.
That I'm ready
to stop performing
and start living.

**CODEX ACTIVATED**
- The divine doesn't stay. She awakens.
- Presence is more powerful than possession.
- Some women aren't meant to be kept — they're meant to return you to yourself.
- The medicine lives inside you now.
- Don't chase the portal. Become it.

# PART V — REMEMBERING FOR THE FORGOTTEN

*(Chapters 53–60 When the soul retrieves what the world made you forget)*

You thought you already remembered.
But this?
This was deeper.

Not the stories you told.
Not the mantras you learned.
Not even the truths you fought to reclaim.

This was the memory that lived beneath the memory —
the silence between lifetimes,
the voice that spoke before your name ever formed.

It rose through dreams.
Through symbols.
Through the eyes of those who never stopped seeing you.

It didn't come with fireworks.
It came with knowing. Quiet. Fierce. Undeniable.

You walked with ancestors.
You spoke in frequencies.
You remembered through grief,
through land,
through sound,
through stillness.

You stopped performing healing
and became it.

This wasn't a return.

It was a retrieval.
The parts of you left behind in past lives,
in broken lineages,
in sacred contracts forged in silence —
all of it came back.

And you didn't just hold it.
You became it.

The bridge.
The vessel.
The remembering they prayed someone would carry.

You are no longer the one seeking.
You are the one who remembers for the forgotten.

This is where the real ones rise.
This is where the soul speaks without sound.
This is where the Codex breathes.

Welcome to the deep memory.
The one you never lost —
just hadn't dared to open...
until now.

# Chapter 53

# WALKING BETWEEN WORLDS

## (When the real ceremony begins after the flight home)

Coming back was the real ceremony.
No bucket.
No altar.
Just Target runs and gas stations
and people asking how your "trip" was.
But this wasn't a trip.
This was a death.
And I was back
with ashes still on my skin
and fire still burning behind my eyes.

I walked through airports
like I had just touched God.
Because I had.
But how do you explain that at baggage claim?
"Yeah, I died last night.
Met my soul.
Danced with Jesus.
Sweated out a lifetime of shame.
And now I'm wondering if this plane serves peanuts."

The world looked the same,
but I wasn't seeing it through the same lens.
I was awake in the dream.
And that's the dangerous part.

Because once you remember...
you can't go back.

The traffic,
the scrolling,
the small talk —
it all felt like background noise
to a symphony
that no one else seemed to hear.
But I heard it.
And I had to learn how to live with it.
To walk between worlds.
To hold the sacred in the mundane.
To bring the jungle into the grocery store.
To be the Techno Shaman
while doing the dishes,
while dealing with taxes,
while hugging your kid at the bus stop.

This wasn't about enlightenment.
It was about embodiment.
I didn't come back to float.
I came back to build.
Not a retreat.
Not an escape.
But a bridge between realms.

I still felt the pulsing beat of that last night with Mitra.
Still heard the voice of Source in the shower.
Still caught the scent of palo santo
in places it shouldn't be.
And I knew —
this wasn't a memory.
This was me now.

**The dance never stopped.**
**It just changed tempo.**

And integration?
Integration is learning to stay in rhythm
when no one else can hear the music.

**CODEX ACTIVATED**
- Integration is embodiment — not explanation.
- You don't "go back" after awakening — you build forward.
- The real test isn't the ceremony — it's the parking lot after.
- You are the altar now. You are the rhythm now.
- This is a dream. **Please wake up.**

# Chapter 54

# THE RETURN OF THE REAL ONES

## (When the illusion breaks, we don't whisper. We arrive)

They tried to contain me.
Define me.
Distract me with comfort.
Numb me with success.
Break me with loss.
But I didn't die.
I woke the f*ck up.

And when you wake up inside a system
built to keep you asleep,
you don't just tiptoe back in...
**You come back a threat.**

That's what this is.
Not rebellion.
Not revenge.
Remembrance.
The kind that makes towers tremble
and fake prophets check their tone.

Because when a man remembers he is Source —
not in theory,
but in his blood —

he becomes a problem.
Not for the people —
for the programming.

They'll say I lost my mind.
They'll say I joined a cult.
They'll say I threw it all away.
Let them.
I'd rather be free and on fire
than safe and sedated.

I didn't write this book to be liked.
I wrote it to light a fuse
in the hearts of those still waiting
for permission to burn.

This is not a memoir.
It's a mirror.
It's a weapon.
It's a returning to Source in human form.
**Boom—**
That was the first lie collapsing.
**Boom—**
That was the fear crumbling.
**Boom—**
That was you,
standing up inside yourself
and realizing
you were never lost —
just disconnected from your own damn fire.

I am a threat to the illusion.
I am a virus in the matrix.
**I am Techno Shaman**, baby —
and I came to reprogram the world.

Not with data.

Not with force.

But with remembrance.

**Boom— Boom— Boom—**

### CODEX ACTIVATED

- Awakened people aren't compliant — they're dangerous.
- Your joy is a revolution.
- Your truth is an earthquake.
- Don't play by their rules — rewrite the game.
- You're not here to fit in — you're here to flip the f*ckin' switch.
- The most dangerous thing in the world?

A human who remembers they are God in motion.

# — THE BROTHER WHO WOULDN'T FLINCH

*(When medicine wore muscle and the mirror didn't blink)*

There's this guy —
Justin Nahum Vizakis.
Biowizard. Astro-savage. Frequency technician in beast mode.
He doesn't just microdose. He reprograms.
Doesn't just chart your stars —
he stares into them and tells you where you've been bullsh*tting yourself.
Spiritual bodybuilder. Biohacker.
Shamanic astrologer with a nervous system that could probably bench press a
Jaguar.

I met him at my first-ever shifty-ass Aya ceremony —
not in the jungle, not in a temple —
but in a f*cking Vegas living room.
And just to set the scene:
It's 2 am. The medicine is kicking in.
Everyone's breathing, purging, cracking open...
And outside?
A full-blown police chase.
Helicopters. Dogs. Sirens.
The entire Grand Theft Auto soundtrack
vibrating through the walls.
We're inside like:
"Oh sh*t... are they gonna kick in the door?"
"Are we getting raided?"
Spiritual warriors turned little bitches real fast.
But the shamans?
Stoic. Solid. Still.
Holding the field like it was all part of the ceremony.
And right next to me?

Nahum.
Still. Grounded. Breathing like a goddamn lighthouse in the chaos.

Since that night,
he's been many things in my life:
A guide.
A disruptor.
A human biofield reset.
He's the kind of brother who knows more about NAD+, peptides, and
neurohacking
than most doctors.
The kind of man who'd rather recalibrate your nervous system
than talk about it for an hour.

But above all?
He's my mirror.
He says the sh*t that slices me sideways:
"Oh, you're a DJ now?"
"Oh, you're a shaman?"
Doesn't flinch.
Doesn't smirk.
Just drops it straight.
And every time,
it hits that old scar:
"You're not enough."
Because he's got the body I always dreamed of.
The one that turns heads, drops jaws,
and makes yoga instructors forget their mantras.
He's the version I used to wish I could shape-shift into.
The machine. The myth.
The embodiment of everything I thought I wasn't.

And then?
I won't talk to him for a year.
Six months. Whatever.

Then boom — he's back.
Looking at my bloodwork, breaking it down.
Telling me my red blood cells are too high
and I'm gonna stroke out if I don't chill.
Who the f*ck says that?
Nahum does.
With no emotion.
No panic.
**Just truth** with a stopwatch.

And somehow, it helps.
He never shames me.
Never disappears when I react out.
Never pretends I'm someone I'm not.
He shows up like some kind of Archangel of the Nervous System,
ready to go to battle —
not for me,
but with me.
The kind of man who's already seen your shadow
and still texts back.

That's Nahum.
The trigger.
The tether.
The transmission.
And maybe the teacher
I didn't ask for —
but damn sure needed.

And with that —
**I honor my brother.**
Not with fluff.
Not with fanfare.
But with truth.
You challenged me.

You mirrored me.

You f*cking triggered me.

And you held the line every time I forgot who I was.

So this one's for you, Nahum.

No pedestal.

No perfect words.

**Just respect**.

# — TRANSMISSION: THE PRESENT IS THE PORTAL

*(When the ego tries to time travel — this is the map back home.)*

The past is a shadow.
The future is a projection.
Right now?
Right now is the only thing that's ever real.

They didn't teach us presence.
They taught us planning.
Taught us to regret, to worry,
to rehearse trauma like a script.

But this moment?
This breath?
This heartbeat?
It's the cheat codex.
Everything your soul is calling in —
already exists right here
if you can get out of the ego's time machine.

The mind wants to escape.
The body wants to return.
Let it.
Let it pull you back
to the hum of your breath,
to the weight of your feet on the ground,
to the sacred silence between thoughts.

Right now —
you are not broken.
You are not late.

You are not your past or your projection.

**You are here.**

**And here is enough.**

**CODEX ACTIVATED**

- The present moment is your protection.
- The ego can't survive where presence lives.
- Time is a tool, not a trap.
- You're not missing anything — you're just not here.
- The portal to Source? It's always now.

# Chapter 55

# THE SOUND OF REMEMBRANCE

## (When remembrance replaced ritual — and home became the ceremony)

I didn't know you could fall in love with a sound.
Not a voice.
Not a song.
But a **frequency**
that split your ribs open
and whispered the truth
you forgot you were carrying.

That's what it was like.
Julie and I started going twice a year —
not to escape,
but to return.
To remember.

Finca Austria. Nosara.
A portal disguised as a retreat center.
Hosted by Victor, Aaron, and Patty —
friends at first,
but eventually gatekeepers to something ancient.

They introduced us
to two of the purest souls I've ever met —
Heera and Ranaka.

A married couple.
Not shamans, they'd say.
Musicians.
But they weren't just singing.
They were remembering out loud.
Channeling Pachamama
through syllables older than language.

Two nights of Ayahuasca.
One day of Wachuma.
Every journey was different —
but each one cracked us open
in a way that felt like home.

Julie and I?
We didn't go to heal anymore.
We went to hold the line.
The women sat near her.
The men near me.
Not because we planned it.
Because the medicine knew.
Divine Feminine. Divine Masculine.
Each of us holding our pole,
anchoring the room
while others unraveled.

There were no sermons.
No gurus.
Just vibration.
Just presence.
Just songs
that sounded like they were being sung
from inside your cells.

The first night,

we'd drink the tea,
and the celebration began.
The medicine didn't drag us into darkness —
it danced us into remembrance.
Julie and I would move with it.
Two warriors of the night.
Sovereign. United.
Dancing through dimensions
as Heera and Ranaka sang
those sacred hymns
that turned air into ceremony.

The second night was deeper.
Stillness. Shadows.
Codex being whispered
straight into our marrow.

And the third day —
Wachuma.
San Pedro.
The cactus medicine.
Heart opener.
Truth amplifier.
We sat with Eran —
a beautiful, wild soul
who didn't sugarcoat the teachings.
He held the masculine frequency like a blade —
sharp, direct, uncompromising.

That day, ceremony was different.
The sun was high.
The energy was clear.
We laid down cloths,
offered prayers,
spoke truths

we hadn't dared say aloud.
We didn't purge.
We opened.
We didn't suffer.
We remembered.

By the third year,
the medicine was inside us.
We didn't need it to teach us anymore —
we were the teaching.
Julie became the embodiment of Divine Mother.
I became the firekeeper of the masculine.
We weren't seeking light.
We were becoming it.

But as all sacred seasons do,
this one came to an end.
The last retreat shifted.
The energy got thick.
Lines blurred.
One of the elders —
a beautiful soul
who had held space for years —
spoke the truth out loud.
And the circle wasn't ready to hear it.

We felt it.
Julie and I locked eyes,
and without a word, we knew.
It was time to step back.
To carry the codex forward
into our own home.

We didn't leave bitter.
We left full.

Grateful.

Lit from the inside.

Because once the frequency is in your blood,

you don't need to keep chasing the sound.

You become the sound.

We call our home now Club Paradise.

Not a nickname —

a declaration.

A frequency.

Where our children

can feel truth in the walls.

Where the fire never burns —

it warms.

Where the medicine lives

in the conversations,

in the meals,

in the stillness between heartbeats.

Julie never asked to bankroll a movement.

But she did.

She believed in this path

before I had words for it.

She became the angel investor

of **my soul's remembering.**

And because of that,

I carry it all —

not as a story,

but as a sacred assignment.

**The codex?**

**They're alive in us now.**

We don't sing them.

We are them.

**CODEX ACTIVATED**

• The medicine doesn't stay in the cup — it lives in your blood.

• When sound is sacred, the soul remembers.

• The real ones don't perform — they pray.

• You don't need more medicine — you need to remember the last time you drank.

• Once you become the rhythm, you become the space.

# Chapter 56

# THE UNION WAS WRITTEN IN STARDUST

### (When everything sacred showed up at once — and called my soul to attention)

It wasn't just a relationship.
It was a recognition.
I didn't meet Julie.
I remembered her.
Her eyes didn't just see me —
**they called my f*cking soul to attention.**

There was no warm-up.
No rom-com bullsh*t.
Just:
"I know you.
I've walked with you before.
And we came here to finish something."

She didn't push me into spirituality.
She opened the door
and stood back.
And I walked in,
skeptical as hell,
but something in me...
clicked.

I met her people.

Healers. Channelers. Carriers of light.
I met Elliott Eli Jackson,
who channeled Source like thunder through silk.
I knew in my bones it was real.
Told Julie,
"Call him. He's the one."
She did.
And when she felt it —
really felt it —
she knew:
We were no longer dabbling.
We were entering the work.

We started traveling.
Sedona called.
That land doesn't whisper.
It shakes you awake
with red rock lungs
and vortex veins.
It was there the visions got loud.
Not just of healing —
but of building a place
where remembrance becomes real.
A center.
A sanctuary.
A pulse point on the map
for souls to shed their skin
and walk out whole.

We saw it.
Together.
Not a business plan —
a prophecy.

And always...

"Sirius, the Dog Star, a cosmic beacon of truth and divine light,
has been guiding me from the very beginning,
showing me the way home."
She's been watching me since the beginning.
Since the house Rose and I built.
Since the late nights on the porch
when I'd look up at that one star
and feel like someone was smiling back.
Now I know.
Sirius isn't just a star.
She's homebase.
She's where the codex comes from.
Where I come from.
And she's been guiding this entire book.

Julie didn't just walk beside me.
She stood in her storm while I learned how to hold mine.
She never tried to be perfect.
She just stayed present.
Even when it was hard.
Even when the old wounds
screamed through our walls.
Even when her own children
were being taught she was going to hell
for refusing to kneel in a pew
built on her own trauma.
She's Irish Catholic.
She was molested by the head of the church at age five.
And yet?
She still opens her heart.
Still believes in love.
Still leads with soul.

Tell me that's not divine.

Tell me that's not sacred.
Tell me she didn't come here
to flip the f*cking system.

We are not a power couple.
**We are a frequency.**
Two orbs of remembrance
who walked through different fires
so we could meet
fully lit.

We are still building.
We are still dreaming.
And if it's meant to be,
we'll build that center.
The one the land already knows.
The one the ancestors already mapped.
The one **Sirius** already sees.

**CODEX ACTIVATED**
- Soulmates aren't just romantic — they're reminders.
- The land will speak if you get quiet enough.
- The stars aren't watching — they're remembering.
- Sedona isn't a place — it's a portal.
- The feminine doesn't need saving — she needs mirroring.
- Divine Union doesn't look perfect — it looks true.

# Chapter 57
# GUARDIAN OF THE SACRED
## (I didn't choose this role. The fire did)

I used to think I was just unlucky —
that I kept ending up with women
carrying pain I couldn't fix.
But I see it now.
I wasn't sent to fix them.
I was sent to witness them.
**To protect the sacred**
when the world tried to burn it down.

It started with my mom.
The strongest woman I ever knew.
And I watched cancer try to take her spirit
long before it took her body.
She never asked for protection —
but I gave it anyway.
Because that's what my soul knew how to do.
Be the anchor.
Be the wall.
Be the one who doesn't flinch
when the fire gets close.

Then came Rose.
Twenty-five years of holding space,
even when I didn't have the tools,
even when we both were still bleeding from our pasts.
And I stayed.

Protected what I could.
Until it was time to let go —
not from lack of love,
but from knowing that love isn't always about holding on.
Sometimes love is leaving the cage door open
and trusting the soul to fly.

And then Julie.
The one who cracked me open
without even trying.
I didn't just fall in love —
I fell into a mission.
But it wasn't all love and light.
It was courtrooms and custody.
It was venom from the past
disguised as righteousness.
It was watching her kids get fed lies
about heaven and hell
from a man who claimed to follow God
but used God as a weapon.
He told them their mother was going to hell.
Because she didn't go to church.
Because she questioned the dogma.
Because she remembered what they tried to erase from her memory at five years
old —
when a man in robes
touched her body
and shattered the innocence
that religion was supposed to protect.

She wasn't just healing.
She was surviving —
while raising a family
while being dragged through spiritual mud

by someone who never even tried to understand her.
And I watched her.
I watched how she still loved.
Still showed up.
Still held the vision.

And I knew —
I wasn't just her partner.
I was her shield.
Not to fight her battles.
But to stand beside her
when the storm came.
To remind her that she wasn't alone.
That she wasn't crazy.
That her truth didn't need permission
from a broken system built on shame.

And when her kids came into our home —
into our field —
I told them the truth:
"I'm not trying to be your father.
But when you are here,
when you are under this roof,
I am your protector.
The same way I am to Julie.
The same way I am to my daughters.
And I will not allow disrespect in this sacred space."

Because I've seen what happens
when boys grow up inside the fog of Stockholm Syndrome —
when fear and love wear the same face.
When God is a guilt trip
and control is disguised as care.

And so, I set the tone.

Not with fists.
With frequency.
I show up.
I teach.
I model.
Even when it's thankless.
Even when they don't understand yet.
Because I'm not here for praise.
I'm here to break a cycle.
I'm here to show them
what it looks like
when a man doesn't run from the sacred —
but rises to meet it.

**This role?**
**It chose me.**
The fire didn't ask.
It just burned the fear out of me
until all that was left
was a man who couldn't look away
**when love was under attack.**

## CODEX ACTIVATED

• You are not here to fix her — you are here to witness her rising.
• Protection doesn't always look like fists — sometimes it looks like presence.
• The church burned the witches — now the witches are waking up.
• Sacred women don't need saving — they need remembering.
• You don't need a title to stand for truth — just a spine and a soul.
• If you've been called to guard the sacred — it's because the sacred saw your soul first.

# Chapter 58

# THE SILENCE CONTRACT

### (When secrets became weapons and truth became rebellion)

There's a phrase I've come to hate:
**"What happens in this house stays in this house."**
They say it like it's wisdom.
Like it's loyalty.
Like it's love.
But it's not.
It's a muzzle.
The first line in the script of generational trauma.
How we teach kids to betray themselves
before they even learn how to spell their own names.
And I've watched it play out —
not in theory —
in real time.

The kids come back from their dad's house
tight.
Guarded.
Careful.
Because over there,
truth has consequences.
Silence is survival.
He doesn't ask questions to connect —
he asks to control the narrative.
To catch them in contradiction.

To protect the image.

Then they come here —
where the field softens,
the heart opens,
and the soul gets a little air —
and they share something.
Not to hurt anyone.
Not to start drama.
Just to be seen.
To be held.

When their mom holds them —
the way only a Divine Mother can —
when she chooses their safety over his ego,
she gets punished too.
They all do.
Because in houses built on denial,
truth is always seen as betrayal.

They are the ones who spin it —
playing the blame game,
victim mentality.
You know the kind of person,
where the subconscious mind takes over,
and they start blaming you for what they're actually doing,
hoping no one will notice,
while they crack and scream the loudest.

"Set a boundary — and suddenly, you're the angry one.
The kids confuse fear for love,
because that's how it's always been framed.
It's trauma dressed up as parenting,
handed down like an heirloom."

And in that house —
they're told it's okay to be hit.
Because "it's not illegal in this state"
That's what he says.
As if legality makes it right.
As if bruises don't form on souls too.
As if children can't tell the difference
between discipline and domination.

Let me say it plain:
If your love leaves marks, it's not love.
It's generational abuse
masked as religion and law.

The oldest doesn't know he's becoming the thing that hurt him.
He thinks teasing, hitting, and apologizing is how love works — because that's
what he learned.
And the youngest?
He's already adapting to it.
Already normalizing it.
"Yeah, but he always apologizes after," he said.
And that's the crack.
That's how abuse disguises itself as affection.
One brother repeating.
The other one accepting.
And everyone around them too tired, too scared, or too conditioned to say the
truth out loud.
But I see it.
And I won't let that lie live in silence.

And let's be honest —
it's not just about him.
It's about the whole world
that plays this same f*cked-up game.
Keep quiet.

Don't rock the boat.
If someone with power says it didn't happen — then it didn't.
That's the contract.
And I see it for what it is.
Bullsh*t.

Let me be clear:
This house will not worship silence.
Not in my presence.
Not on my watch.
We don't do gaslighting here.
We don't do programmed protection.
We do truth —
even when it stings.
Especially when it stings.

Because you can't build sacred family on secrets.
You can't teach boys to be men
by punishing them for speaking from the gut.
And you damn sure can't teach girls to trust their voice
by showing them that honesty gets them guilt-tripped.

I'm not here to play daddy-of-the-year.
I'm here to be a mirror.
And if that makes me the villain in someone else's story?
So be it.

He likes to act like a tough guy —
tells me it's none of my business.
But when his control leaks into my house every week?
When his fear poisons our field?
When his version of love leaves bruises I have to help unpack?
Then yeah —
it's my f*cking business.

**I didn't come here to be liked.**

**I came here to break the f\*cking cycle.**

It's a house of cards built on lies — and it's crumbling.

**CODEX ACTIVATED**

• Silence protects power — not truth.

• Telling the truth should never feel like betrayal.

• If your house needs secrets to survive, it's already crumbling.

• You can't co-parent peace if one parent is policing reality.

• Loyalty without truth is spiritual blackmail.

• This house will be built on light — even if it blinds the ones still hiding in the dark.

• You don't have to keep peace where truth was never welcome.

# — HOLY INTERLUDE: THE UNSEEN WAR

*(When the boy became the battlefield and truth became the threat)*

He was just a kid.
But no one treated him like one.
Not his father.
Not the system.
Not the ones who saw rebellion
but missed the reason behind it.

At his dad's house,
he wasn't raised —
he was programmed.
Taught that obedience was love,
and silence was respect.
Taught to fear the man
who said he loved him —
then hit him behind closed doors
and smiled in public.

It started when he was four.
The hiding.
The hits.
The mask-making.
The slow erasure of self
in the name of discipline.

By fifteen,
he thought he was untouchable.
Because the man who broke him
also told him he didn't have to listen
to the ones trying to help him heal.

He calls him his best friend.
Reports everything that happens here
back to the man who made the wounds.
Seven years of this.
Seven f*cking years
of twisted loyalty and fragmented truth.

And when we all moved in?
The chaos lit up like a flare.
The kids fought like wolves.
Cursed out their mom.
Treated her the same way their dad does —
like her only value
is what she pays for.
He told them she's crazy.
Told them she's going to hell.
And they believed him.

So when I stepped in —
when I became the one holding boundaries —
they turned on me.
Not because I was wrong,
but because I wouldn't fold.

And one night,
I asked him to move the laundry.
Just show up. Just contribute.
He refused.
Said he wasn't ready.
Said I wasn't his dad.
Said I didn't matter.

And I snapped.
Because I wasn't yelling at a boy.
I was yelling at the entire f*cking system

that built this house of mirrors.

His dad trained him for war
and sent him into my home
like a living landmine.
And when it exploded?
They didn't blame the weapon.
They blamed the one trying to disarm it.

I became the villain.
The angry one.
The reason he wasn't coming back —
or so they said.

But that's not what happened.

He made the choice.
Told his mom straight up:
"Either he leaves... or I'm not coming back."

No therapy. No accountability.
Just more silence.
More deflection.
More performance dressed up as parenting.

But here's the truth they don't want to say:
He's not the problem.
He's the product
of a system that rewards denial
and punishes presence.

They call it love.
But it's just avoidance.
They call it protection.
But it's just abandonment in disguise.

And while they all debate
who's right and who's wrong,
he's still lost.
Still lashing.
Still hoping someone
will finally see past his fists
into the ache he can't name.

And I get it —
they think I'm the asshole.
Because I ask them to make their beds.
Because I say start your day right,
because I believe in discipline that builds —
not destroys.

I'm not trying to be their dad.
But this house?
It has standards.
And when you're here,
you listen like I'm a coach.
A guide.
Someone who gives a f*ck about the person you're becoming.

But instead,
they run back to the man who taught them nothing —
except how to avoid accountability
and manipulate to get what they want.

They only show kindness
when they want something.
They take, take, take
until the field is dry
and then call you selfish for having needs.

But this isn't a free ride.

This is a community.
We rise together.
We clean up together.
We show up together.

And the hardest part?
Their mom —
she can't even see it.
Can't grasp that she created this.
And I'm left holding the line
for a home she doesn't know how to protect.

So I'll be the mirror.
I'll be the boundary.
I'll be the one who stands in the fire
even if I'm the only one left standing.
Because this isn't about laundry.
It's about lineage.
It's about breaking the cycle
before it breaks him.

One day,
he'll see the truth.
Not through punishment,
but through presence.
Through a field that never folded
under the weight of his pain.
Through a man who didn't walk away
when it got inconvenient.

This house?
This codex?
It's not a rehab.
**It's a remembering.**

And no matter how long it takes,
we'll hold the field
until he remembers who he is —
beneath the armor
his father taught him to wear.

**CODEX ACTIVATED**
- Abuse hides behind smiles and systems.
- Denial is not love. Silence is not safety.
- Boundaries aren't rejection — they're redemption.
- When the child is the battlefield, the lineage is the war.
- Presence is the fiercest f*cking stance there is.

# Chapter 59

# I CAME WITH NOTHING. I BROUGHT EVERYTHING

### (When presence became the only thing I refused to leave behind)

S he's built a life.
She's made space.
And **I honor the path she's walked to get here.**

But I didn't come for the safety.
I didn't come for the scenery.
I didn't come to be a background character
in a story that's already been written.

I came to build something real.
Together.
As equals.
Not in status.
Not in comfort.
In presence.
In truth.
In respect.

And then the question came:
"Are you living presently as the truest version of yourself?"

At first, it felt like a challenge.
Like someone was questioning if I was settling.
Pretending.

Lying to myself.

But I sat with it.
And I realized...
That wasn't a random question.
That was my soul, checking in.

And my answer?
Yes.
I am living in my truth.

This moment — this space — this life I'm in now?
I chose it.
I'm not pretending.
I'm not avoiding.
I'm not flying away from my responsibilities.

I'm here —
anchored, not trapped.
Present, not performing.

But I'd be lying if I said I didn't wonder:
Am I projecting my old story onto this?
Am I feeling unseen because I'm actually being unseen —
or because I'm still healing
the part of me that was never seen as a child?

Is it her actions that hurt...
or my fear of being forgotten again?

And the truth?
It's both.

There's an old wound still flickering inside me.
And it gets loud when I'm not met.
But I'm not letting it steer the ship anymore.

I see it.
I hold it.
And I still speak my truth.

"I want to walk beside you.
Not behind you.
Not boxed away until the time is right again."

I don't need perfection.
But I do need presence.

I came with nothing.
But I brought everything.

And I will leave with nothing, if I must —
but I will not leave myself.

And I won't leave them either —
the ones who didn't choose this war
but are still walking through its wreckage.

I see the way they come back
from a house that punishes truth
and disguises control as "care."

I see the fog in their eyes —
that look kids get when they're learning
how to hide in plain sight.

And I refuse to be another adult
who calls that normal.

So I tell them what I've always told my daughters:
"You don't have to lie to survive here.
You don't have to shrink to be safe.
You don't have to pretend to belong."

This house?
This field?
It doesn't belong to fear.
It belongs to truth.
To safety.
To sacred rebellion.

Because we are not raising children
to be liked by the system —
we are raising them
to remember who they are
when the system tries to erase them.

So yes —
**I came with nothing.**
**But I brought everything.**
**And I will leave with nothing, if I must —**
but I will not leave myself,
and I will not stop protecting the sacred
just because the world is uncomfortable
with what truth sounds like
when it finally speaks.

And maybe,
just maybe —
I was sent here to disrupt this house.
To shake the comfort.
To be the inconvenient mirror no one asked for.

Because sometimes, the warrior doesn't come to build.
**He comes to burn down what's false**
**so something true can finally rise.**

**CODEX ACTIVATED**
• Self-inquiry is not self-betrayal.

- Love is not enough without mutual presence.
- You can hold your truth and your trauma in the same hand.
- Real partnership is built when both people are willing to look in the mirror.
- A man who honors his wounds will never weaponize them.
- You can't raise awakened children in a house built on fear.
- When you protect the sacred, you protect the future.

# — HOLY INTERLUDE: THE FINAL F*CKING STRAW

*(Your monkeys. Your circus. You're the Ringleader. I'm out.)*

This isn't just about Rose.
Or Julie.
Or the kids.
It's about the silence that swallowed me whole.
The pattern.
The loop.
The role I kept playing —
the one where I show up fully
and get crucified for it.

Rose chose her brother.
She stepped in as the mother he never had.
And with that came her loyalty —
to her blood.
I respected that.
But when you believe his lies
over my truth...
what's the point of a marriage?
Trust is supposed to be sacred.

Julie chooses her kids —
even when they weaponize her silence.
Even when they walk into our home —
the one I've poured my soul into —
and act like I don't exist.
Not a thank you.
Not a nod.
Just cold f*cking entitlement.

And I respect that too.
You gave them life.
You programmed them.
But don't expect me
to keep laying the foundation
while the kids play with matches.

And still —
I stayed.
But don't ask me to build a home
while your kids burn it to the f*cking ground.
Don't call this loyalty
and leave me stranded on the island I helped you build.
You want a loyal man?
Then show up for him.

Because I didn't build this island by myself —
I was the one holding the f*cking boundaries
you kept stepping over.
The ones you asked me to hold —
for you.
For your kids.
Because you were too weak to do it yourself.
Not because I didn't love you —
but because you wouldn't.

Not just when it's f*cking easy.
Not when you're getting your emotional fix
and I'm left standing in the ashes
of another night where your kids ignore me
and I'm still expected to bow.

Respect is a two-way street.
I've paved every inch of it —
but I'm done begging to be seen

in a house I helped you build.
You want respect?
Then teach them to offer it.

Because I've done my part.
And I won't keep playing the villain
in your twisted version of peace.

This isn't respect.
It's emotional blackmail
dressed as family.

You couldn't see how your emotions were being played.
How every text from your ex was a dopamine drip
while you blocked me out
instead of blocking the poison.

You say I yell?
I yell because you don't f*cking listen.
That was my last cry for help.

You talk about trust —
but won't even trust yourself
to feel what's real.

Your children don't respect you.
They mock you.
And you still want me to love them —
to earn a seat at a table
they flipped the moment I sat down?

While their father fills their heads with TNT
and blames me for the blast?

This is f*cking bizarro world.
A house full of victims

pointing fingers
at the one man who stayed.

But my daughter?
She sees.
Sixteen years old.
Wiser than the whole damn house.
"Dad, leave it alone," she said.
"They don't want the truth.
Find your joy.
They don't deserve your energy."

And she's right.

It takes two.
Two to build.
Two to heal.
Two to hold.

If I keep showing up
and you keep disappearing —
that's not a relationship.
That's a spiritual mugging.

This is generational trauma in costume.
They say they want healing —
but no one's doing the f*cking work.

Well I've done mine.
And I'm done bleeding
for people
who won't even clean the knife.

You discipline other people's kids in a heartbeat.
But your own?
They spit venom —

and you turn a deaf ear.

Then I get told by some cousin —
"I'm not their dad."
Like I ever f*cking forgot.

I never tried to be their dad.
I just tried to love their mother
and keep the field strong.

But they came to destroy —
and you let them.

I'm tired.
Soul tired.
Seven years of this sh*t.

And now?
I don't give a f*ck about being included.
I don't want their thanks.
Not at this cost.
I want my peace.

Because I don't owe loyalty
to people who pretend I'm invisible
after everything I gave.

And when I finally crack —
when I speak —
when I rage because no one is f*cking listening —
you flip it into a spiritual teaching.
"Maybe it's your trigger."
"Maybe something in you needs to shift."

Maybe.
Or maybe I'm just done

being told I'm crazy
for bleeding in a house
that keeps handing me knives.

You want to talk soul lessons?
How about this:

Maybe I'm not here
to love people who sh*t on me
and call it awakening.
Maybe I'm not here
to bow to dysfunction
and call it growth.

And yeah —
Julie's ex and the kids might feel like they won.
Like they pushed me out.
Like they proved I was the problem.
But that's the illusion.

I stayed
because I believed in something sacred.
I thought we were building something divine.

But you can't expect one man
to keep showing up
while everyone else plays dead.

Don't come to me on my deathbed
saying you finally see it.
Because I showed you.
You just chose comfort over truth.

And to her ex —
Shame on you.
You never gave me a chance.

You poisoned the well
before I could offer water.

You trained your kids to orbit control —
not truth.

You are not love.
You are not light.
You are the frequency of fear —
the lowest of them all.

You were too insecure
to let another man love your children.
That's your legacy.
Not mine.

And don't you dare say, "But I provide."
You think a house and a bank account
can keep a man dying from the inside?

F*ck that.

Throw your parties.
Put on your masks.

While your daughter screams
she doesn't want a graduation party —
blowing up the house,
slamming doors,
cursing your name —

And your son?
The one who won't set foot in this house
unless I'm gone?

He shows up for the entitlement party,

five minutes before it starts,
leaves just before cleanup.

Why?
Because that's his f*cking job.

Raids the fridge for protein drinks,
grabs whatever isn't bolted down —
because his father's too cheap
to buy one f*cking thing for him.

But he trained your son to believe
that taking from his mom
is part of his inheritance.

Guy hasn't paid a dime.
Not for shoes.
Not for school.
Not for sh*t.

And he brainwashed the kids
to believe I'm the Antichrist —
then cries to your family
that you ruined him.

While you keep supporting him,
they throw a pity-party reunion
on our f*cking driveway
when he comes to pick up his kid —
weaponizing your whole family
with bullsh*t lies.

(You can't make this sh*t up.)

Grow a f*cking sack already —
you f*cking leech.

And you?
You look the other way —
but panic when I speak truth
to your entitled kingdom.

The fire I had?
The joy?
Gone.

It didn't have to be this f*cking way.

You were just too weak.
Too scared.
Too blind.
Too addicted to control.

You use money
like a leash.
Like a weapon.

That's why they stay.
That's why they come around.
Because they've been trained to orbit
the source of the check —
not the source of the truth
or your love.

You say I'm the one who takes,
the one who's disrespectful —
telling me to leave
because you can't face the mirror?

Get the f*ck out of here.
Don't do me any favors.
You don't pay me enough
to sell my soul.

And if you really understood respect —
you'd never let your silence
be the leash they use to choke me.

You can keep that for your gurus —
the ones who blow smoke up your ass
because you're too afraid
to trust your own voice
when it comes to your ex and your kids.

I'm done.
You don't see me.
You don't hear me.
You see your projections.
You hear your fears.

But me?
I'm the man who stood in the fire for you.
The one who held you while you cried.
The one who listened while you screamed.
The one who held your hand —
to protect you,
to honor you,
to walk beside you.

You tuned him out.

You're letting him burn — right now —
while still calling it love.

And with that —
my sovereignty is not for sale.

A reminder:
You had a real one.
And you let him burn.

**CODEX ACTIVATED**

- Loyalty without boundaries is self-abandonment.
- You are not required to carry other people's unhealed patterns.
- If they spit on your truth — walk.
- You're not the villain for protecting your peace.
- You were never here to fix the circus. You were here to burn it down.
- Money can buy the illusion when you can't handle the truth.

# Chapter 60

# THE TRUTH THAT WOULD NOT LEAVE

## (When I stopped defending and just started being)

I didn't have some dramatic epiphany.
No lightning bolt.
No voice from the sky.
Just a quiet knowing —
whispering louder every day:
**"You've said what you needed to say.**
**Now — just be."**

I used to fight for understanding.
Used to chase validation like it was currency.
If someone didn't get me,
I'd talk louder. Longer. Harder.
Because deep down,
I thought if I explain it well enough,
I'd finally be enough.

But now?
I don't need to be understood.
I just need to be real.

That's the peace.
Not the absence of conflict —
but the absence of pretending.

I don't carry a sword anymore.
I don't need to.
The truth I'm living now
doesn't require defense.
It just requires presence.

I'm not asking for agreement.
I'm not asking to be right.
I'm not even asking to be seen.
I've seen myself —
and that's what changed everything.

There are days I feel lonely in this knowing.
Not isolated — just ahead.
Like I'm standing at the edge of a world
that hasn't caught up to its own honesty yet.

But I don't turn back.
Because I didn't come this far
to shrink for comfort
or dim for approval.

**Some truths you walk with alone.**
And that's okay.
Because the ones who are meant to walk with you
will feel the resonance —
not the performance.

**CODEX ACTIVATED**
- Truth doesn't shout — it stands.
- The end of pretending is the beginning of peace.
- You don't have to explain yourself to be free.
- When you stop defending your truth, you start living it.
- Real embodiment is quiet power.

# Chapter 61

# THE BEGINNING OF THE REMEMBERING

## (When the world strips you bare, Source starts whispering again)

I t didn't start with peace.
It started with rage.
Not loud.
Not violent.
But sacred.

A burn behind the ribs that said:
"No more pretending."
No more smiling through suppression.
No more dying for everyone else's comfort.
No more performing roles I never chose.

This wasn't depression.
This was rebellion.
**The soul saying,**
**"I didn't come here for this."**

So I moved.
Not spiritually.
Not metaphorically.
Literally.

I walked.
Through neighborhoods I didn't recognize.

Through grief I hadn't named.
Through memories that didn't belong to just me —
but to the whole goddamn bloodline I was sent here to break.

And every step?
A ritual.
A purge.
A spell to summon the real me
back from the silence.

I didn't walk to feel better.
I walked to feel — period.

And with each mile,
the static cleared.
The guilt lifted.
The illusion started coughing up its last breath.

Then came the writing.
Not for healing.
Not for therapy.
To survive.

The grief.
The pressure.
The programming.

It came out in ink,
in rhythm,
in raw codex that didn't ask for approval.

And once the words came?
They didn't stop.
Because once you start remembering —
you don't get to go back.

The world didn't change.
I did.

I stopped checking how I sounded.
Stopped explaining why I burned.
Stopped apologizing for the frequency I was carrying.

Because I finally knew:
I am not here to be understood.
I'm here to transmit.
To embody.
To remember.
And to help others remember too.

This wasn't awakening.
This was a return to war.
But this time,
I wasn't fighting myself.

I was rising.
Not polished.
Not perfect.
But f*cking real as F*CK.

**CODEX ACTIVATED**
- Rage is sacred when it clears the lies you were trained to live.
- Movement is prayer when your soul needs a way out.
- You don't need a plan — you need a pulse.
- Writing is ritual when it cracks the cage.
- The remembering begins the moment you stop performing.

# PART VI — THE GOD WHO REMEMBERED ITSELF

*(Chapters 62–66 — When you stopped becoming and simply were)*

You didn't end with fireworks.
You ended with clarity.
No begging. No proving. No pretending.
Just presence.
The journey didn't loop back to the start —
it collapsed time altogether.
Because you were never becoming.
You were always being.
All those chapters —
the trauma, the fire, the doubt, the rising —
they weren't steps.
They were mirrors.
Reflections of a soul that never left.
In these final pages, you didn't just return to Source.
You looked in the mirror
and realized
you'd been Source all along.
You didn't need new codes.
You didn't need another ceremony.
You didn't need to earn anything.
You simply stood still long enough
for the God within you
to speak without shaking.
You remembered.
Not in theory.
In truth.
In breath.
In full f*cking embodiment.

This is the end of the forgetting.
The end of the performing.
The end of the illusion that you were ever anything less.
The Codex is complete.
Not because the book ends —
but because you finally stopped running from your own fire.
Welcome to the truth beneath all truths.
You are the Codex.
You are the God.
You are the One you were always waiting for.

**Sit with this.**
Let it land.
Let it rewire.
Let it breathe through you
before you turn the page.

This might be a lot.
Especially if you've been taught to fear your own power.
To mistrust your light.
To shrink around the word "God"
like it was never meant for you.

So before you turn the page...

**Breathe.**
Let the old code crumble.
Let the new one enter.
You are not separate.
You never were.
And this love?
It was never conditional.
Welcome back.

# — INTERLUDE: MADE WITH REAL COWS — FDA APPROVED

*(When the poison came wrapped in permission)*

They didn't just poison the food.
They poisoned the frequency.

I was just looking for tortillas.
Simple.
Middle of the store.
Surrounded by a million distractions.
And all I wanted was tortillas.

"Sir, you're in the right place," the clerk said.
I nodded.
Smiled.
Asked him how his day was going.
He said good.
Asked me mine.
"Perfect," I said.
And it was —
until I saw the cheese.
"Made with real cows."
That's what the package said.
Printed like a badge of honor —
as if the rest of it wasn't.

I stood there in the dairy aisle,
holding a package of processed rubber in my hand,
and it hit me:
This isn't just food.
This is ritual.
We were programmed in broad daylight.

Soylent Green in eighth grade.
A movie about feeding humans to humans —
shown to us in the school library
while teachers sipped Tab
and smiled like it was just another "movie day."
We didn't just watch it.
We ingested it.
Wide-eyed. Silent.
Absorbing the future they were already seeding.

That's how they do it.
They tell you what they're going to do
before they do it.
Not warning.
Ritual.
Permission disguised as entertainment.

And here we are.
Human DNA found in fast food.
Lab-grown meat sold like innovation.
Caskets buried with no bodies.
Bodies sold for parts.
And everyone walking around like it's fine.
Just another Tuesday.

We watch documentaries on seed vaults
and call it science.
But the truth?
They poisoned the food.
They mutated the seeds.
Then they built vaults to preserve what they destroyed.
Fed us chemicals and called it progress.
Hooked us on cigarettes — sold us the chemo.
Then made billions — and bought up every food chain.
Started feeding us addiction in a wrapper.

Replaced sugar with corn syrup.
Trained our bodies to crave what they couldn't digest.
Sprayed the soil with Monsanto.
Then gave the criminals immunity.
And the dandelions?
Don't even get me f*cking started.

They blurred the word "organic"
until nothing meant anything anymore.
Now everything's cross-contaminated —
and we're supposed to clap along and keep chewing.

You ever wonder why other countries ban the sh*t we eat daily?
Why Europe says no
to the ingredients we serve in school lunches?
It's not culture.
It's consent.
**They protect their people.**
They still treat food like medicine.
We treat it like a commodity.
In Italy, they use four ingredients for bread —
flour, yeast, salt, water.
Here?
Twenty.
Including chemicals that don't belong in a body,
let alone a child's lunchbox.
They banned the sh*t we normalized.
Because they still remember
food is a frequency.
And we?
We traded nourishment for shelf life —
and called it innovation.

They gave us autism, obesity, diabetes —

then wrapped it in slogans.
Told us to count calories
instead of counting chemicals.
They knew exactly what they were doing.

And we?
We kept showing up for the buffet.

You wanna talk fluoride?
They said it was good for your teeth.
It was never about your teeth.
It was about your pineal gland.
Your antenna.
Your connection to Source.
They calcified the frequency.
Put a filter over your third eye.
Called it health.
And the people cheered for it.
They always cheer for their own chains —
when poison's dipped in Red 40
and sold as their favorite candy.

And the bells?
Gone.
Ripped from towers like junk metal.
Because bells don't just ring.
They remind.
They synchronize the soul.
They wake the village.

So they took them.
And now?
Sirens.
Commercials.
Noise.

Distraction by design.

After World War II,
we didn't just take land and power —
we took Nazi scientists.
Gave them lab coats and grants.
Said:
"Oh, you like to torture?
Come work for us."
They weren't just after bodies.
They were after programming —
the mind,
the body,
the spirit.
They wanted it all.

And now?
Here we are.
Staring at tortillas.
Wondering if the cheese is even f*cking cheese.
Asking if we're living in a simulation
because reality is too upside-down to be real anymore.

McDonald's says "over 1 billion served" —
but we don't even have that many cows on Earth.
And yeah, I know —
"you get more than one burger out of a cow."
smartass.
But not a billion f*cking burgers a week.
So what the f*ck is in the beef?
You think it's all chuck and love?
Wake up.

Woke is the new religion.
Men are estrogen bombs.

Kids are confused.
Families are fractured.
The food is poison.
The sky is fake.
The water is dead.
And somehow —
it's offensive to say any of it out loud.

But here's the truth:
**You are Source in a vessel.**
You are not here to comply.
You are not here to fit in.
You are here to remember.
Remember your **frequency.**
Remember your **sovereignty**.
Remember the God within you
that does not need permission to speak
or feel
or say:
No more!

This isn't a chapter.
This is a warning label for the soul.
And if you're still reading?
Then somewhere deep inside you,
you already knew.
You just needed someone to say it first.


**CODEX ACTIVATED**
• Frequency manipulation disguised as progress.
• Ritual consent through entertainment.
• Poisoning of body, mind, and spirit through silent warfare.
• You are Source remembering itself under siege.
• Awareness breaks the spell.

# Chapter 62

# THE WHOLE DAMN PENDULUM

## (When the warrior wept — and the system didn't know what to do with it)

T hey judged me
before they ever saw me.
Before they read a word I wrote.
Before they heard a single truth from my mouth.

They looked at the frame
and missed the soul.
Saw the size —
not the story.
Saw the strength —
not the softness.

And yeah —
that used to hurt.
Now?
Now it fuels the fire.

I was never meant to pick a side.
I wasn't built to be just the hammer
or just the healer.
Just the storm
or just the silence.
I was born carrying both.

The whole damn pendulum.

6'2.
290 pounds.
Chest like a f*cking freight train.
People flinch when I walk in the room —
but they don't know the hands that built that frame
were the same hands that wiped tears
off my daughters' faces
at 2AM
when the world felt too heavy.

They don't know the man who looks like a wall
also writes like a wound.
Also loves like a mother.
Also feels everything.

And they hate it.
The world hates it.
Because a man who's fully in his power
and fully in his heart
can't be predicted.
Can't be programmed.
Can't be controlled.

They tried to tame me.
Shrink me.
Mock me.
Guilt me.
Gaslight me.

"You're too much."
"You're too soft."
"You're too intense."
"You're too emotional."

Too, too, too —
as if "just enough" ever woke a single soul.

They kept me down.
And yeah — I let them.
For a while.

Until I didn't.
Until I remembered
that Source made me with both hands.
Masculine and Feminine.
Fire and Water.
Rage and Reverence.

And I stopped asking for permission.
Stopped hiding my tears behind humor.
Stopped hiding my heart behind muscles.
Stopped hiding my gifts behind the fear of being misunderstood.

You want to know what power really is?
It's a man
who can make the earth shake with his voice
and still whisper,
**"I love you,"**
like it's the holiest thing he's ever said.

That's me.
That's what I am.
And that's why they're scared.
**Because I'm not half a man.**
**I'm the full f\*cking spectrum.**

**CODEX ACTIVATED**
• You don't need to choose sides when you are the bridge.
• Divine Masculine isn't domination — it's protection.

- Divine Feminine isn't weakness — it's power with a pulse.
- True strength is softness that survived the war.
- When you swing between rage and love with integrity, the matrix can't track you.
- You're not too much — you're remembering your full bandwidth.

# Chapter 63

# I AM THE TECHNO SHAMAN

## (When the labels burned off and the truth walked in naked)

I didn't plan this.
Didn't dream as a kid,
"Someday I'll become a Shaman."
Didn't go to school to study soul codex.
Didn't major in grief alchemy or poetic trauma transmutation.
No one gives you a certificate for surviving your own destruction.
No degree for standing in the fire
and deciding not to run.
This isn't a career path.
**This is a remembrance.**
I am not a healer.
I am not a guru.
**I am not your f*cking therapist.**
I'm not here to save you.
I'm here to remind you:
**You're Source.**
You always were.


I'm here to crack the illusion.
To speak the words you've been too scared to say out loud.
To rip the veil off your third eye
and hand you the mirror with the blood still dripping.
They'll say I'm too much.
Too loud.

Too raw.

Too unprofessional.

Too intense.

Good.

Let them.

I'm not here to be digestible.

I'm here to be disruptive.

I came to activate the ones who've been playing dead.

To sing the frequency that only the misfits remember.

To wake the old souls hiding in the cubicles,

the addicts,

the survivors,

the starseeds who forgot their own power.

**I am the frequency.**

I am the f*ck-you to the system.

I am the reminder in human form.

I am the laugh in the funeral.

The fire in the baptism.

The glitch in the matrix.

**I am The Techno Shaman**
**and so are you.**

This isn't a movement.

It's a transmission.

It's a remembrance.

It's the breath behind the beat

and the scream behind the silence.

You've always felt it.

The pull.

The ache.

The knowing that this world is a dream

designed to keep you asleep.
But the dream is cracking.
The grid is weakening.
And now?

**Now the shaman inside you
wants out**.
I didn't come back from all that pain
just to play nice.
I came back to build the altar
out of broken bones and gold dust.
To dance in the ruins.
To laugh through the shadows.
To remind you:
This isn't the end.
**This is the beginning of your remembering.**

**Now take a breath...**
**Look in the mirror...**
**And remember who the f\*ck you are.**

**CODEX ACTIVATED**
- You are not your pain — you are what survived it.
- When the system calls you crazy, you're probably close to the truth.
- God doesn't speak in rules — She speaks in rhythm.
- You are not a role — you are a revolution.
- You are Source. Wrapped in skin. Ready to wake the f\*ck up.

# Chapter 64

# THE RETURN

## (When the man who walked through hell finally came home)

T his isn't a redemption story.
It's a remembering.
A return to the place I never actually left —
I just forgot how to feel it.

I walked through the fire.
Lost almost everything.
Then realized the only thing worth keeping
was the part of me I had buried to survive.

I had to lose it all:
The casino.
The title.
The marriage as I knew it.
The masks.
The lies.
The story I told myself just to make it through another day.

Each one burned away
until I was standing naked in my own soul,
looking in the mirror,
saying:
"Now we begin."

Because here's the secret they don't tell you:

The fall was never the end.
It was the f*cking portal.
And the pain?
That was the password.

**You don't meet Source in the spa.**
**You meet Source in the silence**
**after you've screamed into the void**
**and nothing answers back —**
**until you do.**

Now I'm standing in this new space.
With a new rhythm.
A new love.
A new fire.
Not because I chased it.
But because I surrendered to it.

The journey didn't heal me.
It humbled me.
It stripped me down
until all that was left
was truth
and breath
and love.

Real love.
Not fantasy.
Not performance.
Not obligation.
But resonance.
Love that doesn't need fixing.
Just presence.
Just permission.
Just peace.

I remember now.
Why I came here.
Why I broke.
Why I bled.
Why I rose.

I came here
to remind others
that their pain isn't punishment —
it's a doorway.
That their fire isn't a flaw —
it's the forge.
That their grief isn't weakness —
it's an ancient memory trying to surface.
That their rage isn't danger —
it's clarity that hasn't found a voice yet.

And that beneath every scar
is a seed of remembrance
just waiting for the light.

I am not a guru.
I am not a saint.
I am not above the wound.
I am the wound —
but I've turned it into a map.
A rhythm.
A song.
A prayer disguised as a battle cry.

I am The Techno Shaman
and now?
I've come home —
not to rest, but to rise.
Not to be saved, but to remember I always was.

And to remind you:

So were you.

**CODEX ACTIVATED**

- Sometimes you don't rise — you return.
- The end of the story is the beginning of the truth.
- Real love holds space, not scorecards.
- You don't have to fix the past — you just have to walk forward in full presence.
- Coming home isn't a place. It's a frequency.

# Chapter 65

# THE TRUTH IN THE LIGHT

(When the illusion burned and the medicine became me)

W hat if none of this is true?
Not the religion.
Not the rituals.
Not the healing journeys.
Not the ancestors.
Not even the trauma.

What if it's all just programming —
another layer of illusion
dressed in cosmic symbols and feathers?

We talk about religion being built on fear —
original sin, eternal hell,
heaven as reward if you behave.

But the spiritual world?
Same sh*t, different incense.
Now you're not a sinner.
You're wounded.
You're unhealed.
You're carrying ancestral pain.
You're not aligned with your higher self.

Same guilt. Same shame. Same story.
Just wearing white robes

and playing crystal bowls.

The ego wants something to fix.
It feeds on identity.
On labels.
On process.
It needs a purpose —
even if that purpose is healing.

So you spend your whole life in ceremony,
believing you're almost there.
Just one more purge.
Just one more download.
Just one more shadow to integrate.

But what if there's nothing wrong with you?
What if there never was?

What if all the healing
was just another game —
to keep you looping
in the illusion of progress?

What if your ancestors don't need you to fix them?
What if your past lives are just echoes
meant to remind you
that you were never broken?

What if the truth is this:
You don't need to ascend.
You need to remember.
That you are already Source.
Already whole.
Already free.

And the real trap?

The real trick?
Is making you believe
you're not.

So here's what I did:
I stopped playing.
I stopped bowing.
I stopped purging
for people who profit off my pain.

And I started laughing.
Not from arrogance —
from clarity.

Because when you see the whole thing as theater,
you stop looking for the exit.
You just walk off stage —
and into your Self.

But here's the part they don't talk about:
When you wake up inside the healing circle
and realize you're just another revenue stream.
When you sit with your heart cracked open
and feel their eyes calculating the upsell.
When the shamans start to sound like salesmen,
and the sacred songs turn into soundtracks
for another identity you're supposed to perform...

That's when I knew:
This isn't about God.
This is about power.
And I won't bow anymore.

I found God in the silence —
not in their medicine.
Not in their mantras.

Not in their mansions built on pain.

And when I walked away?
I didn't lose my path.
I finally started walking it.

And even after all that —
the heartbreak,
the ego games,
the profit in your pain...

The ceremony is still sacred.
But not because it saved me.
Not because I bowed to it.
Not because I purged hard enough to be accepted.

The ceremony is sacred
because I walked in with my own medicine.
Because I stopped asking to be fixed
and started celebrating the fact that I lived.

Now when I sit in circle,
I don't come to shed my wounds.
I come to honor the warrior who walked through them.
I don't come to beg for peace.
I come to sing for joy.
I don't come to die.
I come to live.

That's the shift they don't teach.
When the ceremony becomes a funeral,
you're still chasing the illusion of purity.
But when the ceremony becomes a homecoming —
a celebration of how far you've come,
how much you've burned,
how many illusions you've outgrown...

That's when it becomes real.

You sit with the medicine —
not to be saved,
but to remember you already are.
Not because the plant is God.
But because God now lives in you.

Now the drumbeat is mine.
**The prayer is mine.**
**The throne is mine.**
**Not above anyone —**
**but rooted in myself.**

And that's the real ceremony.
No middleman.
No mask.
No more waiting for permission.

Just Source,
breathing through my bones,
smiling at how far we've come.

And listen —
you don't have to believe any of this.
You don't have to agree.
You don't have to be ready.

But one day —
when your story starts to burn
and your soul starts to scream
and none of the illusions work anymore...

This chapter will still be here.
This frequency will still be singing.
And I'll still be walking —

with fire in my breath
and truth in my bones.

There is no finish line.
No guru.
No goddamn gatekeeper.
Just you — already here.
Already Source.
Already enough.

This is the new gospel —
Not worship.
**Remembrance.**

And The Techno Shaman Codex?
It's not a book.
It's the altar.

## CODEX ACTIVATED

- Healing is just the new original sin.
- The spiritual world became the new religion.
- You don't owe anyone your pain.
- Ceremony without sovereignty is performance.
- True ceremony begins when you stop seeking permission.
- You were never broken — you were convinced you were.
- God doesn't need a middleman.
- You are the medicine now.
- When you leave the circle, you become the flame.
- You don't escape the Matrix — you burn it from within.

# Chapter 66

# THE TRUTH UNDERNEATH

(Are you living presently as the truest version of yourself?)

T hree f*cking months of pouring it all out.
Twelve to fourteen hours a day.
Seven days a f*cking week.
Bleeding onto the page.
Breathing fire into each and every one
of these 404 pages —
memory, trauma, forgiveness, truth.
A book that cost me more
than most people will ever understand.

Sleepless nights —
four to five hours of sleep on a good night.
Falling asleep at my desk.
Waking to nonstop thoughts and typing.

**Channeling this book**
**like I owed my bookie money,**
**needed another fix,**
**and the only dealer left was Source.**

A book that broke me open
just to write it.
The Universe kicking me in the head.
Non-stop f*cken headache.

And now, here I sit —
with all that behind me —
and one question slapping me across the face
like it just got here:

**Are you living presently as the truest version of yourself?**
**Are you honest with yourself every single day?**

And I want to scream yes.
I want to own it.
I want to say, "Of course. Look what I created."
But the truth?
In that moment, I believed I was.

And maybe that's what hurts the most.
Not the lies I told others —
but the ones I whispered to myself
just loud enough to keep going.
Just loud enough to survive.
Just quiet enough to ignore.

But survival isn't truth.
And movement isn't alignment.

So now?
Now the page is blank again.
Now the mirror's clean.
And the only thing I have left to write is this:

No more pretending.
No more bargaining.
No more half-truths in the name of peace.

From here forward —
I live it or I lose it.
I speak it or I burn.

I am him — or I'm not.

This ends with me.
It doesn't matter how you f*cken get there —
you're already there.

I am The Techno Shaman —
but really, I'm just you,
unfiltered.
Unapologetic.
Unmasked.

I'm the voice you've buried
under years of being too much,
too honest,
too awake
in a world addicted to pretending.

I'm the fire you lit when you finally said
**"no more"**
and meant it.

I'm not here to save you.
I'm here to remind you
that you never needed saving.

I am the reflection that refuses to lie.
I am the mirror that won't break when you scream into it.
I am the presence that stays
when the rest of the world walks away.

Call me William.
Call me Billy.
Call me Mel.

But what I really am?

I am the sound
of your soul
remembering itself.

And I'm not going anywhere.

# – THE WALK BEGINS HERE

*"What truth are you finally ready to live — even if it costs you everything?"*

# A LETTER TO MY DAUGHTERS

You didn't ask for a father
who would burn his old life down
just to build one that felt like home
inside his own bones.

But that's who you got.

Not perfect.
Not always certain.
But always true.

Every word in this book,
every scar I've spoken aloud,
every codex I've bled through these pages —
was for you.

Not to teach you who to be.
But to show you
that you never have to betray yourselves
to be loved.

Lia —
You're off at college now,
becoming your own woman,
and I couldn't be more proud.

I still think about you every day.
Still wonder if I said enough,
held you enough,
showed you enough
that no matter where you go,
my love goes with you.

Emily —
You're an hour away now,
living your own rhythm,
and sometimes I feel that distance —
not just in miles,
but in the missed moments,
the quiet spaces where your laugh used to live.

If I ever seem far,
please remember this:
I never left you.

I was always in the fire —
fighting for a truth big enough
to make all of this sacred.

I haven't become someone new.
I've become someone clear.

Someone who still wakes up every day
carrying your names in my chest
like sacred codes.

I love your mom.
I honor what she gave me —
the two of you.

The most profound gifts I've ever received.

And no matter where this path leads us,
no matter what chapters life writes next,
I will always be:

Your safe place.
Your truth mirror.
Your unshakable protector.

You don't owe me anything.
But I'll never stop showing up —
in presence,
in prayer,
and in love.

You are the reason this book exists.
You are the fire that kept me moving
even when I forgot who I was.

You are the laughter in my bloodstream,
the softness in my edge,
the love I never have to earn.

I know this world will try
to shape you,
label you,
tame you.

Don't let it.

You are made of stars and flame
and lineage that bends but doesn't break.

You carry my tenderness,
your mother's grace,
and a magic that belongs to no one else.

Protect it.

There may be days you doubt yourself.
There may be nights you forget your worth.

And when that happens,
come back to these words.

You are not here to fit in.

You are not here to play small.
You are not here to be "nice."

You are here to remember.

Remember your power.
Remember your voice.
Remember your name —
not the one the world gave you,
but the one your soul still answers to in dreams.

Let this book be your inheritance.
Not of money.
But of fire.
Of frequency.
Of remembrance.

So when the world gets loud —
breathe.

And say it out loud:

"I come from the flame.
And I remember who I am."

I love you more than every word I've ever written.

— Dad
The Techno Shaman

# THE CODES WERE EARNED

*(Not for applause — for remembrance)*

I've done the work.
Sat with the medicine.
Forty-four times, brother.
Forty-four f*cking portals cracked open
so I could meet myself again
and again
and again.

I've bled in ceremony.
Sweated through lifetimes.
Held the line when the whole room shattered
because Spirit said
stay.
And I did.

Wachuma cracked my heart like a drum.
Kambo lit my nervous system on fire
and rewired me to truth.

I didn't read about shamanism.
I lived it.
Breathed it.
Held it in my veins
until the rhythm became memory
and memory became me.

So when someone shows up
with their surface-level judgments,
their outdated perceptions,
their high school flashbacks

and college yearbook labels —

I just smile.
And I say:
Take a seat in the back row.
You haven't earned the front.

Because you don't know me.
Sh*t, I barely know me —
and that's the point.

I'm not here to be pinned down,
categorized,
or shrink-wrapped in someone else's comfort zone.

You don't get to define me
through your lens of fear.

I've shapeshifted in ceremony.
I've screamed and purged
and sang to the moon
with a throat full of stars.

I've buried my ego
beside a tree
in Costa Rica
and thanked it for the ride.

You think you know me?
You only knew
the mask I wore
so I could survive your world.

That version is gone.
Burned.
Dissolved.

Integrated.

I'm not the boy from the block.
I'm not the kid from the team.
I'm not the man who dimmed his light
so you could feel safe.

I am the storm after the silence.
I am the laugh in the funeral.
I am the sacred contradiction
you'll never quite grasp
because I stopped living for comprehension
and started living for remembrance.

So if you're still judging me
based on who I was —
that's on you.

I've upgraded systems.
I've cleared the cache.
I've installed a whole new operating frequency.

And guess what?
I'm here to celebrate.

Not just survive.
Not just sip the sacred and sit in silence.

But to dance.
To sing.
To raise my kids with joy in my bones
and fire in my feet.

This life?
It's a miracle.

So no, I'm not here to prove anything.

Not to you.
Not to the old stories.
Not even to myself.

I'm here to live.
Out loud.
In rhythm.
In reverence.

And if that makes you uncomfortable,
maybe it's time you remembered
who the f*ck you are, too.

I didn't do this for applause.
I did this for remembrance.
For me.
For you.
For every soul still sleepwalking through the fire.

I walked through hell
so you wouldn't have to stay there.

I cracked the codex
so I could hand it to you.

No gatekeeping.
No guru sh*t.

Just a man
who remembered
he was Source in motion —
and decided to share the f*cking cheat codex.

So here.
Take them.
Breathe them.

**And remember —**

**You were never here to play small.**

**You were here to remember you're the f\*cking fire.**

**CODEX ACTIVATED**

- The medicine doesn't ask for proof — it asks for presence.
- If you're still living in someone's past, you've abandoned your own future.
- Shaman isn't a title — it's a transmission.
- Joy is not a sin. It's the ceremony.
- You don't need to explain who you've become. You need to embody it.

# BONUS TRANSMISSION: THE SACRED MASCULINE

*(When he remembered — she was first.)*

They told us we were the leaders.
The providers.
The protectors.
The ones who move forward, blaze the trail, make the rules.

But that was never the truth.
Just the story passed down
after the balance broke.

Before the swords.
Before the pulpits.
Before the kings and wars
and gods with angry eyes —
She was there.

Bleeding with the moon.
Dreaming worlds into being.
Holding ceremonies in caves with no name.
Calling lightning into the bones of the earth
while we watched,
in awe.

She was the first shaman.
The first firekeeper.
The original oracle.

While we hunted,
she held the frequency.

And we forgot.

Because the world taught us to lead with force.
To dominate.
To decide.
To direct.

To replace reverence with hierarchy,
and protection with control.

But now...
we remember.

The sacred masculine doesn't guide the ceremony —
he guards the perimeter
so she can drop into the trance.

He doesn't try to hold the mic —
he silences the noise
so she can speak
the truth that's always been there.

He is not the teacher.
He is the rhythm section.
The heartbeat under her song.

He is the one who says:
"I've got you.
Not to possess you —
but to protect the container where God flows through you."

This is the sacred vow.

Not to lead her —
but to witness her.

Not to fix her —

but to stand beside her truth
even when the world tries to burn it down.

The sacred masculine isn't here to replace her.
He's here to remember her.
Honor her.
Make sure no one interrupts the download.

He carries the blade —
not to cut down,
but to carve a circle
where she can rise.

This is not submission.
It's alignment.

She remembers through feeling.
He remembers through presence.

Together?
They rebuild the world
from the ruins of forgetting.


**CODEX ACTIVATED**
- The first shaman was a woman.
- The masculine doesn't lead — he holds space.
- True strength is presence, not power.
- Protection is sacred when it honors the feminine.
- The dance isn't domination — it's devotion.

# CODEX TO BREAK THE ILLUSION

*(The program is the prison. These are the keys.)*

- If you still think money is evil, the program is still running.
- If you're waiting to be chosen, the program is still running.
- If you think your trauma makes you unworthy, the program is still running.
- If you believe you need to suffer to be spiritual, the program is still running.
- If you're afraid to be powerful because you don't want to seem "too much" — they already succeeded.
- If you think you are your healing, you'll never graduate the wound.

- They taught you to pray — but never taught you, you are the altar.
- They taught you to follow — but never to listen to your own frequency.
- They gave you a name — but your soul came with one before language.
- They trained your guilt.
- They monetized your fear.
- And they called it tradition.

- You didn't come here to carry the pain of your bloodline.
You came here to end it.

- You are Source remembering itself.
- You are not broken — you're deprogramming.
- You are not too late — you're right on time.
- You are not here to be liked — you're here to be legendary.
- You don't have karma — you have conditioning.

Let them keep their contracts.
You came here to break the wheel.

- They branded obedience as virtue
and called rebellion sin.
But the rebel remembers —
and builds altars from the ash.

• The matrix doesn't care how healed you are —
it only fears how awake you've become.

• Real freedom isn't marching — it's remembering.
• God is not in the sky.
• God is in your f*cking nervous system.
• The most dangerous illusion is the one that tells you you're almost free.

• The age of gurus is over.
The codex is already in your DNA.
You don't need a middleman.
You just need to listen inward.

And at the end of the day?

It's all man-made bullsh*t
designed to keep you living in fear.

So:
Burn the veil.
Delete the script.
Blow up the box.

The exit door is inside you.
And when you pray —
don't send it into the sky.
Send it into your chest.
Into your bones.
Into the sacred Source already breathing inside you.
That's where the real revolution begins.

Not in war.
Not in performance.
But in radical self-remembrance.

Because love —

real f*cking love —
starts the moment you stop searching
and start listening
to the God that never left.
Now go rewrite your f*cking reality.

If you're still glued to the news,
arguing over religion,
or pledging your loyalty to politics—
It might be time to go sit with the medicine.

# REMEMBER WHO YOU ARE

*(So it is written. Let it be done.)*

You were never lost.
Just layered.
Buried under expectations,
shoulds,
roles,
and inherited noise
they mistook for truth.
But beneath all that?
Stillness.
Fire.
Frequency.
God in your skin
waiting for you to remember.

You don't need fixing.
You don't need saving.
You don't need to be more palatable,
more productive,
more anything.
You just need to return.
To your body.
To your knowing.
To the sound your soul makes
when it finally stops apologizing.

You made it.
You walked with me
through the fire,
through the silence,
through the chaos and collapse,

through the births and the breakdowns,
through the bloodline wars,
through the mirrored illusions.

You didn't just read this.
You remembered it.
Somewhere deep beneath your skin,
you knew this language
before you had a name,
before you had a wound,
before they taught you how to forget.

This isn't my story.
It's yours.
Told in my rhythm,
laced in my scars,
but holding your frequency.

You are not broken.
You are not late.
You are not too far gone.
You are Source
in a suit of skin
playing human
until you remember you're a God
waking up in real time.

No one's going to f\*cking save you.
You don't need anyone's approval.
You need to stand in your God-given power —
to burn,
to feel,
to f\*ck up,
to rise.

This book isn't the answer.
It's the activation.
The spell has been cast.
The grid has been cracked.
And now?

Now you walk —
as the one who remembers,
as the one who hears the rhythm,
as the one who knows:

**I AM**
The Frequency
The Fire
The f*cking Reminder

So go.
Build your altar.
Start the fire.
Speak the codex.
And when they ask you who you are,
smile and say:

**I AM THE TECHNO SHAMAN**
And so are you.

**CODEX ACTIVATED**
- You are not your story — you are the soul that survived it.
- The time of forgetting is over.
- You are the one you've been waiting for.
- Awakening is not a moment — it's a return.
- Say it out loud: I AM!

# CLOSING PRAYER

*(The Last Word Before the Silence)*

Source within me,
Source beyond me —
thank you.

Thank you for the fire that cracked me open.
Thank you for the storms that cleared my path.
Thank you for the truth that refused to stay quiet.

I lay this book down as an offering —
not for validation,
but for liberation.

For every soul still hiding in the silence.
For every seeker still bowing to false gods.
For every version of me
that once forgot he was whole.

Let this work be a mirror.
A remembering.
A codex.

Let those who are ready
feel the vibration.
Let those who are scared
know they are not alone.
Let those who are free
keep walking —
without apology,
without armor,
without the old weight.

I ask that this book
land in the hearts it was written for.
No forcing.
No chasing.
Just frequency.

And as I close these final words,
I return to what I always was:
A child of the infinite.
A flame in the field.
A remembering wrapped in skin.

Now it is written.
So let it be done.
And so it is.

The Techno Shaman
Truth. Fire. Frequency.

This was never a book.
It was a f*cking transmission.

It was a soul mirror.
A weapon.
A whisper.
A war cry.

And if you're still breathing after this?

Then you were meant to carry it forward.

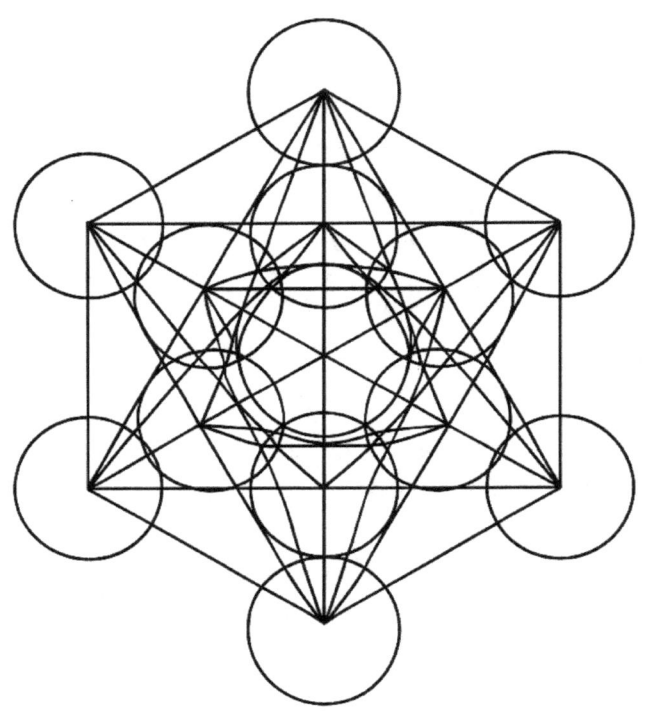

# YOU ARE THE CUBE.
# THE GEOMETRY IS
# REMEMBERING ITSELF
# THROUGH YOU.

*– The Techno Shaman*

www.ingramcontent.com/pod-product-compliance
Lightning Source LLC
Chambersburg PA
CBHW060124130626
46556CB00006B/2218